~~~~~A GUIDEBOOK~~~~~
PEARLS OF WISDOM FOR A HOME SWEET HOME

*ART OF MEANINGFUL
HARMONIOUS INTEGRAL LIVING
WITH HOLISTIC INNER LIFE
UNDERSTANDING*

DADA KRUPA KARUNA

BALBOA.
PRESS

A DIVISION OF HAY HOUSE

Copyright © 2014 Dada Krupa Karuna.

All rights reserved. No part of this book may be used or reproduced by
any means, graphic, electronic, or mechanical, including photocopying,
recording, taping or by any information storage retrieval system
without the written permission of the publisher except in the case
of brief quotations embodied in critical articles and reviews.

A special thank you to Punita Desai for the design of the book cover

Balboa Press books may be ordered through booksellers or by contacting:

Balboa Press
A Division of Hay House
1663 Liberty Drive
Bloomington, IN 47403
www.balboapress.com
1 (877) 407-4847

Because of the dynamic nature of the Internet, any web addresses or
links contained in this book may have changed since publication and
may no longer be valid. The views expressed in this work are solely those
of the author and do not necessarily reflect the views of the publisher,
and the publisher hereby disclaims any responsibility for them.

The author of this book does not dispense medical advice or prescribe the use
of any technique as a form of treatment for physical, emotional, or medical
problems without the advice of a physician, either directly or indirectly. The
intent of the author is only to offer information of a general nature to help
you in your quest for emotional and spiritual well-being. In the event you use
any of the information in this book for yourself, which is your constitutional
right, the author and the publisher assume no responsibility for your actions.

Any people depicted in stock imagery provided by Thinkstock are models,
and such images are being used for illustrative purposes only.
Certain stock imagery © Thinkstock.

Printed in the United States of America.

ISBN: 978-1-4525-1827-5 (sc)
ISBN: 978-1-4525-1826-8 (e)

Library of Congress Control Number: 2014912586

Balboa Press rev. date: 08/19/2014

ON BEHALF OF –

HOLISTIC SCIENCE CHARITABLE
RESEARCH FOUNDATION
HSCRF
206 S. ILLINOIS AVENUE
OAK RIDGE, TN 37830
USA

AND

HOLISTIC SCIENCE RESEARCH CENTER
VITRAG VIGNAN CHARITABLE
RESEARCH FOUNDATION
MAHAVIDEH TEERTH DHAM COMPLEX,
NAVAGAM, KAMREJ CHAR-
RASSTA, N. H-8 SURAT-394185
INDIA

About Shri Dada Bhagwan

Master Holistic Guide

Mr. A. M. Patel, a contractor by profession is devotionally, popularly known as Dada Bhagwan. In 1958, at a railway station in Surat, he spontaneously attained a state of self-realization and became enlightened. He attained a supreme "state of being" distinctly and absolutely separate from his mind, speech and body faculties as an impartial 'observer' from within. He carried within him infinite spiritual prowess that culminated in this singular event in 1958.

Although all those who knew him, will attest to his impeccable integrity of character prior to his enlightened state manifesting. He had a treasure chest of virtues within him that allowed him to live seamlessly as a son, brother, spouse, businessman, son-in-law and all the roles that life demands with zero conflict throughout his lifetime. He was a true Master in the art of living holistically and integrally through Holistic Science. He was searching for the answers to life's puzzles and that treasure chest of wisdom based on His experience resided in his very heart center.

His simplicity and straightforward answers to life's burning questions is refreshing and easily understandable. He was not seeking followers, hence, the question - answer format. He simply existed in that "state of being" and was perfectly contented in that inner state of spontaneous bliss. He did have a deep inner desire to see the people of this world be alleviated from senseless pain and suffering that he saw through his inner holistic vision globally throughout his travels worldwide. So, through the question - answer conversations or dialogues, his timeless wisdom revealed itself spontaneously and naturally.

His most striking legacy is his self-realized followers (*Mahatmas*) who have experienced first-hand his unforgettable pure unconditional love that pierces to the core of the heart center and spontaneously heals wounds and scars in our hearts. He has left timeless footprints in the hearts of thousands around the globe who were fortunate enough to meet him and blessed with identical self-realization.

About Shri Kanudadaji

Present Holistic Guide

Mr. K. K. Patel, devotionally known as Kanudadaji, is a direct link of the Science of Holisticism and Absolutism known as 'Vitrag Vignan'. He is the torch bearer of this freshly revealed radiant rewarding inner science. He is a living lyric of pure love. In his benign presence one feels free, with joy surging within and oblivious of one's worldly problems. He is the living song of spiritualism giving solutions to all questions. In him is perceived and experienced the everlasting love and light of "Holistic Vision" - 'Dada Bhagwan'.

Dada Bhagwan has bestowed on him his infinite grace and blessings to carry on the beacon of light of the spiritual renaissance we are now experiencing today. Grown up in the loving lap of Dada Bhagwan and closely associated with Dada Bhagwan, he has turned himself into a beatific, divine and discerning mobile temple of Holistic Science.

He lives his life with thousands of devoted aspiring followers around the globe who do not feel separate from him even for a moment. His state of being is such that allows him to spontaneously and effortlessly reach the hearts and souls of those who have crossed his path. His grace flows incessantly and those who are open to it benefit from that grace! His presence speaks for itself.

The art of living life holistically with peace and harmony as driving forces is a piece-and-parcel of his treasure chest of wisdom based on sheer experience. He truly lives as the universal student and learns from anyone and everyone that crosses his path. His humility knows no bounds.

Even at the age of 84, he continues to relentlessly collaborate with those who lead Jai Sachchidanand Sangh, VVCRF and HSCRF to ensure that the understanding of "Holistic Science" reaches every nook and corner of the globe. Despite physical obstacles, his only wish is to fulfill the holistic vision of Dada Bhagwan to see peace, joy and harmony brought back to the people of this earth.

Contents

Message from Present Holistic Guide Shri Kanudadaji

On behalf of the *Holistic Science Charitable Research Foundation* (HSCRF), this publication is coming into your hands for you to read and experience one-to-one the reasons for and how to avoid conflicts in our lives. As you begin reading the book, do so with not the mind alone, but go down to the very core of your heart to feel the response given by the enlightened holistic master to the questions put forth to him. Such understanding beyond the mind level and coming from within the very core of the inner Self is vital to avoid or resolve conflicts and behavioral tendencies that are prevalent today at all levels-- individual, family, society, national and the world-at-large. In the beginning, questions or objections may come from your mind, but from our own experience do not pay much attention to them but carry on with the reading and reflection within your own self. In the end these questions and objections may turn out to be irrelevant or go away as you sincerely go deep within and understand the true meaning and essence of the words spoken. Those who are ready for inner transformation and their self interest will find the book to be a valuable guide.

We have lived continually a conflict free life for the past fifty-one years till the present age of eighty-four with total inner awareness of our Real Self and letting go of our identification with the mind-body and speech functions. The inner peace and perpetual happiness we have experienced as a result of non identification of our self with our external bodily and mental functions and their content makes a strong case to recommend this guide to those who are eager to live a life free of conflicts and clashes. True freedom can be tasted as the truth and wisdom is revealed throughout the book from the questions and answers.

Our blessings overflow to all of you from the very core of our heart. We wish that everyone tastes and experiences the inner happiness which has always been within us but gone noticed for so long. The guide book will rekindle our thirst and help us to put the inner happiness within our reach. When we begin to lead a life guided by holistic understanding of our inner self and the Unity in Diversity, the transformation is bound to come. The seed of understanding that is sown now will sprout and come alive in its own time. We have only to be firm in our resolve to lead a conflict free life and do the very best under all circumstances. Mother Nature will do the rest for us.

Let God residing in the core of our heart guide us in every action of ours. Let peace prevail in our homes and our planet earth.

Real Self-realized Kanudadaji
Vadodra, Gujarat, India

Message from the Holistic Science Charitable Research Foundation (HSCRF)

Pearls of Wisdom are a practical guide on how to avoid clashes and conflicts in our day-to-day life. We encounter such situations in our homes, work place, and society at large. Home is where our focus should be the most since it is here we have the maximum interaction with people who are close to us both by proximity and relationship. We spend years with them but are unable to understand them! It is also the center of our activities and demands special attention and mindset skill to deal with multiple situations with different personalities. The emphasis on family and how to live and relate to our closest members is discussed in depth in the beginning of the book itself. In the Vision of the Holistic Scientist, Dada Bhagwan's own words: 'Where there is claim there is blame" and the home is the perfect example. Often we say and do things that we believe are in the best interest of our family based on our own interpretation of right and wrong. However, we fail to recognize that our internal feelings play a major part in these decisions and our opinions and perceptions of the external world are bound to be different from other family members.

When we err, it is a sure invitation for conflict and clashes. No one likes others to point out their shortcomings. The intellect and ego refuses to accept it and this again could very well lead to conflicts. In these moments, our ability to reason and act according to what is in our best interest is diminished. Conflicts are unwanted wars. It is an internal process but manifests externally in the form of responses to external stimuli. The internal conflict within us keeps our power hidden to overcome conflicts. Rather than using the internal power to overcome conflicts, we ignorantly use it to create them. No where can it be truer than in marriage. For example, it is not uncommon to forgive or easily overlook our spouse's gravest mistake when love, serenity, peace and positivity prevails inside us whereas when we are disturbed internally we are prone to find faults with the most trivial event.

Conflicts have more to do with our internal state rather than the external factors. Therefore, they have to be tackled in its core and not by attempting to change the external circumstances. Our entire thinking process has to be changed. Science tells us that we cannot use the same thinking that created the problems to solve them. The problem has to be tackled in its core. Today, with so much of distractions, error has become so much a part of our thinking. What is needed is for someone to point it out and present the facts in a proper form and this book is intended for this purpose. This book is not a collection of **do's** and **don'ts** but of the wonderful essence of its holistic approach. Its unique contribution is that it goes to the root of the problem and empowers us with the inner scientific understanding of 'Cause-Effect' relationship to deal with the real life situations. With change in belief and right understanding it will tell us that healing is easier than hurting and it is not in our self interest to hurt others. Therefore beware of conflicts! Our firm resolve, not to hurt anyone by thought, word or deed itself is a giant step, a great scientific 'cause' in the right direction of love, peace, positive and amicable living – natural consequential 'effects'. We have only to resolve internally and remain unshakably determined in it. Nature will do the rest. This is the effortless holistic path where transformation happens from the inside-outward.

Humanity existed from time immemorial and will remain for infinite time with the "Holistic Vision" of amicable and blissful living as part and parcel as its very nature at its very core. However, modernization and the mechanical, materialistic extrovert lifestyle with so many amenities of outer comfort and happiness, we have conveniently forgotten our basic nature, and due to which we have become self-centered, remaining unsatisfied with tons of unfulfilled desires. Look at the other creatures and we can definitely find them at peace. We experience this very well. As it is revealed by Dada Bhagwan, "The more the abnormalities in the basic human living form the more abnormality in Nature. Such abnormality in human - nature relationship, is how we experience changes in the Nature." So, when such an individual emerges, the lost Science of Holism surfaces and nature blossoms again by regaining its pristine glory of "Oneness" viz. love peace and blissful living.

The book presents several examples of conflicts that take place in our daily living. The material presented in the interactive dialogue style, brings out the hidden consequences of our impulsive reactions that we are so accustomed to. Dada Bhagwan's spontaneous response to the questions in itself is a testimony that these are the words flowing from the very inner core of his illumined, self-realized, Holistic internal "State Of Being" and not an intellectual response. Those of us who are aware of this Holistic revelation can testify that the effect of the words spoken is transformational and gets lodged immediately inside. All that is required of us is sincerity and a burning desire to improve and free ourselves from the clutches of our own mistakes [the world]. We begin to live a Holistic life of freedom "in living" and not freedom "from living". There is abundant, unseen Grace in the words spoken of the illumined souls, the Holistic Scientists, who always act in the best interest of humanity and Nature as a whole. Dada Bhagwan exemplified this truth in his simple living and all those who came in contact with him are indebted to him for the wonderful changes he brought in their lives. Although his words may seem to be harsh or not eloquent at times, it is intended to drive home the point so that it gets permanently lodged in our inner self. It is like the fire without the heat.

Natural living calls for a Holistic approach viz. "Live and let live". When every action of ours is viewed and conducted with this as the center point, Mother Nature helps us in our life journey and keeps us in normality. Normal living is synonymous with natural holistic living and what is required is acting with awareness and relying on our heart and common sense more than our self-centered and heady intellect. Holistic Science opens that common sense, which is a divine gift bestowed on us and it is the best weapon to use when conflicting situations arise. We should learn and master the art of using it. It starts with accepting everything 'as it is' and not as we want it to be, which includes our own self. Surprisingly as it might sound, one thing that we all tend to have is the least acceptance of our self. We tend to be most critical of our self. We compare ourselves with others and find ourselves falling short of our expectations. This process goes on inside us all the time, sometimes even without our being aware of it. The pearls of wisdom tell us to accept our mind-body-speech complex as Mother Nature's gift without any judgment but silently strive internally through Natural Holistic approach to use them without the least hurt to the extent possible. Only then will we be able to accept others as they are. When we encounter people or situations that we don't like, by accepting them we can actually save a lot of misery. Wisdom of Holistic Science tells us to accept every unpleasant situation, just as we would a pleasant one by correct understanding without endurance and changing our wrong beliefs. This is because they are transient in nature and are mere outcome of our own doing!! And by doing so, we have already begun the process of resolving it naturally and holistically.

Sincerely yours,

Dr. Radha Krishnan
President, HSCRF
206 South Illinois Avenue
Oak Ridge
Tennessee 37830
USA

Acknowledgements

As you embark upon this journey in reading this compilation, please be prepared to have epiphanies and wonder why you had not thought of it yourself! The Holistic Master Guide, Dada Bhagwan's dialogue with each and every aspiring seeker of answers was originally in Gujarati, a dialect of Sanskrit origin. A humble attempt has been made with the request and blessings of present Holistic Guide Shri Kanudadaji to transcribe that dialogue into English. Utmost care has been taken to keep the integrity of the essence of the Holistic Master Guide Dada Bhagwan's words in the context of how He meant them.

These "live" discourses with aspiring seekers of answers to life's puzzling questions had taken place in the 1980s. He left His physical body in January of 1988 in India. These conversations had taken place in India and in the United States. It is crucial to read each section independently as it is not a continuous conversation. Each section has deep messages about integral living harmoniously with holistic inner understanding as a driving force. It is more beneficial, if you were fortunate enough to meet the Holistic Master

Guide, to picture Him in the "live" conversations. If you did not meet Him, it is intended that the reader is able to visualize the situational aspect of the discussion.

Please forgive in advance for any unintended errors in translation that may be present. It is most beneficial to keep this book handy as a ready reference for situations that arise in life "as it happens".

May answers to the puzzles that arise in daily living reveal themselves to you. It is our intent the insights be helpful to you in drawing your OWN INSIGHTS from the essence of each pearl of wisdom of His holistic inner vision conversations.

The coming together of this compilation in itself has been an amazing journey of grace flowing between heart centers for a common purpose – to make a positive difference in the lives of others through the sharing of wisdom of experience of one who has lived 'that' what most human beings seek to accomplish in their lives including yours truly. It has proven to unravel as a beautiful tapestry of grace at work and hearts in unison!

First-n-foremost, we offer our utmost gratitude to Present Holistic Guide Shri Kanudadaji for the opportunity to be an instrument of His grace for this compilation of pearls of timeless wisdom for living a harmonious meaningful holistically integrated life.

The dedicated, focused attention to editing and offering valuable feedback for this compilation from Shri Lalabhai

Patel Saheb a Banker from India is pivotal for the completion of this guidebook.

Our heartfelt gratitude to Swami Shri Navinanandji, Celibate with Jai Sachchidanand Sangh from India who originally was instrumental in compiling this book in Gujarati (Na Ho Leshmatra Klesha ke Kadhapo – Let there be not even the slightest intimation of conflict or turmoil) published in 2004 and again in 2010 & 2011 with enhanced revisions on behalf of VVCRF and Jai Sachchidanand Sangh.

Also, heartfelt gratitude to Swami Shri Dipakanandji, Celibate with Jai Sachchidanand Sangh and Engineer from India, who has contributed with feedback and editing for clarity of essence and meaning.

Dr. Shailesh Mehta has played an on-going pivotal role in helping us all with HSCRF to better understand holistic inner science and living and has offered his valuable contribution in the form of his Valuable Summary, in gratitude for his dedication, contribution, presence and leadership.

Rajnikant Patel, retired professional, has provided valuable guidance, feedback and input that have helped fine-tune the clarity of the message, in gratitude for all his devoted time and attention.

And, our heartfelt gratitude for the continued support, blessings and devotion of Shri Suresh Patel from Detroit, Michigan who has dedicated his retired life to researching holistic inner science. Also, our deepest appreciation to

Dr. Shri P. C. Parikh Saheb of VVCRF (Vitrag Vignan Charitable Research Foundation in Kamrej, India) and Shri Sudhirbhai Shah Saheb, Worldwide President of Jai Sachchidanand Sangh who offered their blessings, support and dedication for the compilation of this guidebook.

Finally, our utmost humble gratitude to Shri Dr. Radha Krishnan, an engineer by profession from Oakridge, Tennessee, and President of the Holistic Science Charitable Research Foundation (HSCRF), USA for his review, valuable feedback and tireless service and contribution for the completion of this guidebook and to HSCRF.

Instrumentally in His service,
Dada Krupa Karuna

*Dedicated to each and every human being around
the globe for their valuable presence on this earth to
discover the exhilarating and rewarding journey inward
with the understanding of holistic inner science*

About Distressing Conflict
('*Klesha*')

Klesha or conflict is the word that describes the states of mind that hinder our progress on the path to wholeness. So, conflicts sneak up on us, they can run deep, and when we are in the grips of a conflict, they take our peace of mind and replaces it with anxiety and misery.

Klesha literally means taints or afflictions. *Patanjali* notes 5 klesha's in the Yoga Sutras: *Avidya* (ignorance), *Asmita* (ego, selfishness), *Raga* (attachment to pleasure, fear of change, likes), *Dwesha* (aversion to pain, dislikes) and *Abhinivesha* (persistence, stubbornness).

You will see the word "conflict" throughout the book quite often, actually over 400 times! This was the most appropriate "catch-all" translation for the Sanskrit-based word '*klesha*'. However, it is quite a deep and broad term that really is about all the intricate inner workings within the psyche that gives us anguish, anxiety and misery eventually manifesting in conflict on the outside with others.

Some of the common English terms (nouns, verbs and adjectives) that relate and fall under the umbrella of conflicts are turmoil, tension, anxiety, noisy drama, deceit, arguments, taunting, bickering, yelling, screaming, fighting, bullying, hostility, condescension, bitterness, abruptness, torment, petrify, dominate, ridicule, debase, dictate, humiliate, and torture. Some forms of "conflict" are within such as turmoil, anxiety, depression and tension. Other forms of "conflict" manifest as yelling, screaming and fighting. Also, "conflict" includes more serious forms of hostility including tormenting, ridiculing, bullying and torturing.

Unfortunately, whether one is the receiver of hostility or the giver of hostility, there is pain on both sides and ignorance on both sides. It is important to understand that someone who inflicts pain is in pain themselves! The key is to find the solutions to keep those situations from arising in the first place.

That is just some of the incredible, brilliant revelations that are made in the course of these dialogues that took place between Dada Bhagwan and those aspiring to live meaningful lives with clarity of purpose, harmony, peace and joy.

A certain amount of conflict is natural and normal to everyday life, however, when it is above or below normal is when it becomes "distressful" conflict. Thus, there is the use of "distressful" conflict throughout this guidebook in this context.

A healthy, normal level of interaction involves open communication, an aim to conflict resolution rather than perpetuating the cycle of pain and improved relations with one's own self and others as a result.

We can actively rise above conflicts and soar from within with the correct understanding that the Master Holistic Guide gives through His inner vision of life and living integrally from His own pearls of wisdom born from experience.

Through the correct understanding and use of holistic inner life understanding given by the Master Holistic Guide we are able to maximize this amazing gift of human life to "be" the best human we are able and continually move towards becoming 100% human.

How Can There Be Distressful Conflicts In The Home?

Dadashri – There should not be any conflicts in the home. Are there conflicts happening in anyone's home?

Questioner – Of course conflicts do happen, right?

Dadashri – In the homes of truly humane people who recognize the importance of human life and the values and responsibilities of human birth conflicts do not happen, conflicts happen in the homes of selfish and in-humane people. We are inner–focused humane people. How can there be conflict in our homes?

Questioner – But in actuality, it is a fact that conflicts do happen.

Dadashri – It should not happen.

Questioner – All this talk about it should not happen is right, but what about the fact that it does?

Dadashri – So, conflict is such that will stop if the wrong understanding is removed from within.

Our lives can be lived in such a way that the whole world will be dazzled & amazed! We are the children of humane inner focused people; and if we behave and are seen as uncultured, uncivilized people, how disgraceful and unflattering does it look?! We are the humane inner focused people but today have become uncultured and uncivilized only. Have you heard the word 'inhumane'? It's often said, "Just don't even bother talking about him. He is like an offensive inhumane person."

What qualifies someone as humane inner–cultured? Under any circumstances in life and living when there is not any conflict whatsoever deems someone worthy of being called humane inner–cultured.

Insights From Pearl #1

As human beings, we must live as "humane" beings first-and-foremost in the *home* with those closest to us. This is where humanity starts. By understanding that peace begins within us and with us, we can fully comprehend how important it is to have peace, harmony and humane behavior in the home. Everything in our world starts at and within the home and emanates outwardly from there.

PEARL #2

Where There Is Conflict, There Is Fire Burning

What makes-up conflict? The inner self just keeps burning. Even if the fire is extinguished, the inner self does not stop burning. Dear zombie, the inner self, it is not something to be burned. If a cloth is burning, let it burn, but the dear zombie ignites to burn the inner self. All day long this one just keeps engaging in conflicts only. For a little while in places of illusionary infatuation it drowns oneself temporarily then again just keeps burning in the turmoil of distressful conflicts. The whole world is drowned in distressful conflicts only. Today, everyone belongs to the 'clan of conflicts' only. It is forgotten temporarily only due to lecherous dependencies and weaknesses. Otherwise, distressful conflict does not break and if conflict is broken then freedom (*mukti*) dawns.

Today, the tsunami waves of conflict have washed—over *everywhere*. Even while eating there is conflict and if it escalates then the misguided one goes to get poison. Today that one cannot bear the anguish so the poor zombie drinks the poison; so what, from this an end has come? It has only been dragged farther out, and will have to be suffered again multiplied thousands of times worse over! Instead get through the results of your own karmas in this lifetime only! This is solely due to wrong understanding from the core.

Insights From Pearl #2

When we have peace within us, then there is no fire burning inside. Peace comes with serenity. We must accept our lives, our situations, our relations, and ourselves 'as they are' in order to allow healing to take place *naturally*. The correct understanding as to the purpose of living must be acquired. We are here for such a fleeting moment in time, then why waste it away in conflicts within or without? When we understand that conflict starts from within and then manifests on the outside, we can begin the process of finding resolution within ourselves rather than blaming others for our inner conflict. The journey within is the only way to inner peace and true conflict resolution. The journey within is about knowing one's own heart, learning to listen to the heart, learning to listen with the heart and finding peace with oneself within the heart center. The heart holds wisdom. The intellect only serves to show us positives and negatives, but the heart is where wisdom of experience resides and can help us find serenity, peace. Furthermore, knowing and abiding in the heart center will help us to find purpose and meaning for our lives. Reason and discriminate between right and wrong with the intellect, but decide and rule with the heart as the wise have proclaimed. We do not have to wait for a major tragedy in our lives to embark upon this journey. It is the most important aspect of being a human being to know one's own heart well.

PEARL #3

Factories Opened For Creating Conflicts

Conflict–filled living certainly cannot be called human living by any means! Actually, even farm animals do not engage in conflicts. When farm animals have pain and anguish tears spontaneously fall from their eyes, they *do* cry, but besides humans none other ever engage in distressful conflicts. How is it that there are distressful conflicts among humans? Surely there is some serious mistake left over which gives rise to distressful conflicts. Some undetected mistake is definitely left over! The Lord has assertively said that in order to remove distressing conflicts, an enlightened person is not necessary, only a positively *illuminated* intellect is needed. Intellect is such that it has the capability to illuminate the consequences of actions very well. So, with the help of such a positively illuminated intellect one can easily *diffuse* any conflict arising from within.

Surprisingly, look at what is happening today. Instead, of diffusing conflicts we are mass producing factories of conflicts! Furthermore, where in the world can such goods ever be "exported"? If we ask Foreigners, they say, 'We have so much luxury, yet to sleep we have to take so many pills.' They have so much of the gold in the world; they have so much of the wealth in the world, despite this they have to take pills! And that too, it cannot really be called sleep at all. Truly speaking sleep is that which comes spontaneously and naturally. All these pills have made people numb like inanimate objects. The way balm is rubbed to numb the pain right! Likewise, the pain is numbed. My dear, instead of numbing the pain, why do you not just lay there with open eyes and keep observing yourself! Worst come worst (because of the pain) you will stay awake all night?! Rather than numbing your perception with pills, what is wrong in staying awake? How can it ever be okay to numb your perception?

Insights From Pearl #3

Our worst enemy is perverse intellect in living a happy and harmonious holistically integrated life. When we understand this fully, we can begin to make the shift within to cultivate a positive and balanced intellect with regards to living our lives. We can decide how much luxury is truly necessary and contributing to a meaningful and balanced life rather than making it more stressful and anxiety-filled. Life is not meant to be wasted away in the numbness of intoxication of any sort, but rather, to be embraced as an experience in growing ourselves as human beings in the art of living the best lives we possibly can in our circumstances.

With Correct Understanding Distressful Conflict Abated

Our understanding should be such that this mess that has been created, how can it be cleared–up? How can it be like this? All these farm animals are so wonderfully fulfilling their social obligations. What, do they not have wives and children? They have wives, they have children, and they have everything. They take such precious care of their eggs and before gently placing them they prepare the nest. What, they do not have any understanding in them? And these people who have bagfuls of understanding! Bagfuls of brains!! People look for incubators when they have eggs to hatch. Poor fools, why not build a nest for them?! But these brainy ones seek–out incubators, but farm animals know beforehand that they must place the eggs so nests need to be built. They instinctively know their babies hatch from the eggs, afterwards if the nests are destroyed it is okay, but they immediately have instinctive understanding about their eggs. Then in this chaotic harsh age these brainy ones have come! Actually the bags labeled with "brains" when they are opened all that comes out are perverse brains; otherwise, in the world how can it ever be that humans are suffering? Look if you have come into human form and if there is pain in being a human, then how can you call yourself a human? If farm animals do not have suffering, then how can humans have it? Unfortunately, you have not understood your boundaries nor your best interests and you go on blindly walking according to what others say. Furthermore, you keep butting heads with others at every turn. That is what monkeys do! Humans do not go around butting heads; they blend seamlessly with one another. With your own understanding do you not know how deep your pockets are? If your salary is four hundred, then how much is the neighbor's? They say it is ten thousand a month. So, you know that you absolutely cannot let their influence and way of life enter in your home. Do we not understand that if our vision gets twisted then our attitude will get corrupted? So, at home you let your family know that our income is so much and you explain to them that we do not base our standard of living according to that of our neighbors. So, it is certainly necessary to understand everything correctly, isn't it?

Insights From Pearl #4

We have lost the simplicity of living with common sense and naturalness due to *over-exercising* our intellects. We have missed the mark on keeping our intellects in a positive mode despite all the worldly luxuries. The more luxury, the more complaints and apathy! That is not a smart equation for balanced, meaningful, and harmonious living. Taking an honest inventory of our lives, situation, strengths and weaknesses enables us to live our lives within our means in all aspects. Living with practical, common sense is the key for living a meaningful and satisfying life. We cannot allow our minds to be "corrupted" by comparing with others unnecessarily! Our lives are our own. The mind and body we were born with are ours alone. Why allow them to be mortgaged-out to others? It is our experience and it is up to us to maximize the experience as a meaningful, worthwhile life while on this earth. Nature has given us the tools we need to lead meaningful, peaceful, and harmonious lives. It is up to us to make a firm decision and utilize them. This is because what we think and decide eventually happens in our life!

PEARL #5

Tremendous Liability Of Freebees

Unfortunately, you walk in a direction that is not in your best interest. Just because the neighbors get a sofa the wife will say that we should also get a sofa. The wife will *say* you should get a sofa, but should you not ask the wife if she is out to ruin you or what? But the pathetic one does not know how to explain the situation appropriately to the spouse and instead ends up physically abusing them. So, these misguided people are not only abusing their spouses but mentally and emotionally destroying themselves in the process as well. Then they will say they are unable to control their minds. Actually you yourself have abused your own mind. How ironic is it that your own mind is not in your own control?! There should surely be some reason for this, is it not? So, who has corrupted the mind? The children you can be sure are being corrupted by the neighbors! The neighbors will call over the children and say that your dad is like this from the core. Since the neighbors talk badly of the father, the children like the neighbors! The children believe the uncle next door to be cool, but actually the uncle is corrupting the minds of the children. So, the children are being corrupted by others, but how is our mind being corrupted?

There simply is no knowing of whether the mind will stay straight or get corrupted by any given action! What will the poor one say when he is tempted with something for FREE?? It is like having more ice-cream just because you are getting it for free; but in this process your mind is being corrupted. What will be your state of being when the free is gone?! There are so many people that go crazy after free "Brandy". First they go crazy after the free "Brandy'" then end up with a vicious addiction! So, first our people know that it is not worth it to take anything for free in this world. The MOST expensive things in this world are those that are free, so BEWARE of FREE, do not touch. The MOST expensive of expensive, these incredibly liability–filled expensive things that are free should not be allowed in. Anything FREE, it is a colossal liability! And these people have believed free to be fair and called themselves 'brainy'. And they will go around boasting to everyone that they have not spent a dime and their friends have spent it for them. Oh poor one, you are killing yourself, but unfortunately you have no awareness of this! Today, there is no sane sense of awareness about anything. If there is no awareness of liberation (*moksha*) that is not a problem. There really is no awareness of liberation, it is not there from the very beginning; but is it not necessary to have awareness of best-versus-worst self interest in living life at least? What is in my best interest in living and what is not, is that awareness necessary or not?

Insights From Pearl #5

Seeking anything for free results in damaging our quality of life. Why should we seek anything for free? We give away our power of choice as human beings to listen to our inner intuitive senses when we become victims of so-called 'free' things in life. It is smartest to cultivate an inner attitude of self-reliance and living within our own capacity. It is even smarter to cultivate an inner attitude of gratitude for what nature provides to us through our own efforts without "selling-out" or "mortgaging-out" ourselves for things that will cause us to become dependent and weak. There is nothing wrong with taking genuine help from others with the clear intention to repay the debt, but it is foolish to allow ourselves to become victims due to vices and weaknesses. There is a fine line there.

Find A Way Out Of This Trap

At first it was always, 'Let's go see a movie at the cinema.' So they go. Then the wife will test him and say, 'I cannot carry this boy.' Then the guy will say, 'Here, I'll carry him.' Then he will run into some buddies that make fun of him, 'Fool, you have your wife with you that is roaming around with her hands free and you are walking around carrying the boy.' Then he feels embarrassed inside. Then he says to the wife, 'Hey, you carry the boy, now.' Poor fool, what need was there to take her to see the movie? If that lady was begging to go, she may say it, but we know we get snared, now how to solve this dilemma? But, she cannot be encouraged, 'Let's go see a movie at the cinema.' It cannot be said, 'Let's go, let's go.' There was a negotiated contract at the time of marriage, right!

Instead, if that shop is never opened, what is wrong? It is way better to just chill without that shop. After opening this type of a business, it just becomes a trap! How can this be called humanness? Human–ness can be called that when such as Diwali, Christmas or the New Year comes once a year, but the sweetness of the vibrations it generates persists throughout the year. In the whole year, similarly, five days maximum should be such where dilemmas arise and the rest of the days pass–by like a gentle breeze or gurgling brook without any hitches; but there is never ever single day that passes without disturbing drama!

Insights From Pearl #6

Just because everyone does something, does not make it right for us. We certainly can have the insight and introspective thought level to know what is in our own best interest. Depending on what our capacity is, our income is, our way of life is, what our goals are in life, we can *practically* figure-out what is in our best interest as far as our lifestyle and be content with that. Whatever our life is, it can be made a beautiful journey when one makes it one's own life story and does not compare it to anyone else. Life is more important to *experience* for oneself as one's own life experience than to show anyone else or compare with anyone else. It is critical to set one's priorities and boundaries in life for oneself. After all, are we not the stars of our own lives!? Or are we selling-out that precious gift of human existence for money, status, fame or vices? Human life is so precious and fleeting. It is far too valuable to waste away a moment.

PEARL #7

What A Pathetic State Manifests Due To Conflicts!

Now, people immersed in distressful conflict, their minds are battered with anxiety. The mind is battered, the reflective consciousness is battered, and the ego is battered! How can this be called human–ness? Those whose egos are battered and beaten already, how can they be scolded? If you scold them, your breath is wasted. So many have tattered reflective consciousness', they walk around seeing double in their reflective consciousness (in an absentminded state). So many have battered minds, they spend the whole day roaming around in a frantic state, as if the whole world's inferno of fires were chasing them to burn them up!?

Insights From Pearl #7

Human life is far too precious and rare to come-by to waste away in anxiety, distress, and conflicts. The only person we can truly change is ourselves. So, why beat ourselves up or anyone else for that matter? Rather, take the time to care enough about oneself, to know oneself *honestly*. Take an inventory of one's strengths, weaknesses and virtues. Make it a point to accentuate the positives, let go of past grievances against others and forgive oneself first-and-foremost. Then, it becomes possible to maximize this experience of human life as a human being in a meaningful manner. Let peace begin within us through thoughtful analysis of life and what is in our best interest. By avoiding conflicts, we free up so much space and time to maximize the fleeting gift of human life by cultivating our inner virtues and living through the pearls of wisdom discovered on the journey within.

Human–ness Is At Stake, Could Be Lost

Dadashri – Do you like loud noisy drama?

Questioner – No.

Dadashri – Yet, it still happens right?

Questioner – Sometimes.

Dadashri – Diwali, Christmas, New Years only comes on a certain day right? Does it come every day?

Questioner – Then everything cools down in fifteen minutes, the loud noisy drama quiets down.

Dadashri – Take the loud noisy drama OUT of *you*. At whomever's home there are conflicts of any sort, there, in that home, human–ness goes away eventually. It is with tremendous merit karma that human life is attained. There in India people search for clean purified butter (*ghee*) and cannot find it anywhere and you get purified butter (*ghee*) here in the Americas everywhere. If you look for dirty purified butter you cannot find it, how lucky are you! Even with such favorable karma, then shameful, useless misuse happens.

Insights From Pearl #8

The home ought to be a "*home sweet home*". The home ought to be a place where everyone who inhabits that place can relax and be themselves. A feeling of relief, relaxation and peace as soon as one enters into the home marks a "*home sweet home*". What is the need for noisy drama? We all know each other, have committed to living together, then why the noisy hurtful drama? It does not solve anything. Honor the virtues of one another in the home and accentuate them so they will compound and find the scope to blossom nicely just as a plant does with proper nourishment. Where we put our focus on each other is what gets fed! Let's feed the virtues and not the weaknesses and vices; this way a fertile ground for healthy growth with positive encouragement is slowly cultivated in the home for all who inhabit it and enter it. Honest and open communication with kindness as a driving force always heals hearts rather than breaks them. Values involve setting boundaries for ourselves as to what is in our best interest and what is not and living within those boundaries. Ultimately our value system revolves around being the best human being we can possibly be and improve in our humanity as we live-out the remaining journey of our life.

The More Extended Relational Ties, The More Conflicts Arise

Questioner – In India everyone stays in joint families, and the neighbors are in close proximity, and because of all this there is more noisy drama and conflict between husband–wife there; whereas, in America there is only husband–wife only. So, there is an increased adjustment between husband–wife and if the adjustment stays well maintained, it is much better than in Hindustan - India.

Dadashri – That is really great! That is talk that is praiseworthy! If you all are living together in this way; that is a truly great thing.

Questioner – Why is it like that in India (*Bharat*)?

Dadashri – In India the noisy disturbing drama will remain only. To get rid of noisy drama lots of time in close proximity with us (*enlightened spiritual guide*) must be spent; then some people's noisy drama will subside, but noisy drama there in India will not just drastically disappear because there is mother–in–law, grand mother–in–law, and aunt–in–law. Then again the aunt–in–law will complain that this daughter–in–law is not even talking to her. Then the daughter–in–law will tauntingly question that what business the aunt-in-law has with her anyways. She will insist that she is married to her husband. She will demand to know why the aunt has come to their home. She will argue whether she is to be concerned with her husband or concerned with the aunt. Because of this, in India the conflicts and noisy drama easily find their way into the home. There are so many different types of intricate relational ties due to the culture of extended joint family structure.

Insights From Pearl #9

The key to avoid the clashes due to extended family ties is to know when to remain silent and know the inner thoughts of our family members with regards to the various relational ties that the extended family has within it. Each family has a certain code of conduct that is deemed appropriate and it is up to us a member of the family to investigate, understand, integrate and adapt to that code in order to keep peace in the home. Each home is different and has its own cultural code attached to it. It is important to keep an attitude of adjusting everywhere and avoiding clashes in order to keep the distressful conflicts of extended family out of our home environment. If we fully comprehend the importance of peace; our behavior will reflect it with those closest to us. The key is to keep the bond with the immediate family nucleus strong from the heart center. Then, the extended family ties will automatically lose their power to cause conflicts within the home. It is all about priorities. When the people in a home put each other as a priority as far as mentally, emotionally and financially being responsible to and for one another; the chances of another extended family member having the power to break the nucleus becomes much lower. When the family nucleus itself is weak, a family is easily broken by outside forces of extended relations.

PEARL #10

The Lord Does Not Dwell Where There Is Conflict

In this day-to-day life of humans, the men and women of *Hindustan*, how they get through the day, itself is amazing, right?! They manage to pass through so many trials and tribulations. Even so, in the evening after bringing everyone to peaceful resolutions, after settling all the quarrels then the mother peacefully goes to sleep. But until-and-unless conflicts do not go from within the home the *Lord's* fragrance will not be present. As long as there is conflict at any place, till then the presence of the *Lord* will not be there. Wherever there is conflict, the *Lord* is not.

Insights From Pearl #10

The lady of the home sets the tone for the entire household. If she is able to keep an open mind and heart with a clear intention of having harmony, peace and affection in the home; then it sets the protocol for the rest of the family. Complaining is a trigger that has a domino effect and should be avoided as much as humanly possible. A point can be made without complaining! This is where the art of living through practical experience comes in handy. Forgiveness without conditions and unconditional love in the home is definitely helpful in keeping peace, harmony and affection amongst family members. This way the presence of the Lord can be retained within the walls of our home.

PEARL #11

Where There Are Conflicts, There Is No Meaningful Humane Living

Where there are any sorts of conflicts whatsoever, there, at that place the *Lord* is not either. And heart-centered inner living (*dharma*) is not either. Conflict is a pervasive chronic social plague! That from which conflict does not arise is called 'heart-centered inner living' (*dharma*). Eating and drinking beverages in worldly life is not a problem, but that which gives rise to distressful conflict should not be present. What does the *Lord* say? If you do not get liberation (*moksha*) that is okay, but if conflicts do not arise then it is pleasant to live the worldly life. Conflicts are a horrendous plague. It is even a worse plague than Tuberculosis. If conflicts have not gone then you do not even know what heart-centered inner living (*dharma*) is, that is what the *Lord* has said. If there are no conflicts in living, then stay in the worldly life; otherwise seek–out the path to liberation (*moksha*). Where there is even the slightest bit of conflict, there is not heart-centered inner living and where there is heart-centered inner living (*dharma*) there is no conflict *whatsoever*. Conflict can be called a mental illness, because of it, the next life gets ruined. With a physical illness of the body, at least the next life does not get ruined, medicine is taken for it. So, should we not research for a cure or prescription to distressful conflict? For that should there not be an urgent search to identify what has caused the distressful conflict?!

Insights From Pearl #11

Lack of understanding as to one's own best interest in life and lack of self-esteem for one's own self can be drivers for distressful conflict in the home. When a person does not care about themselves, it is impossible for them to truly care for anyone else. We must take the time to understand ourselves and each other as human beings in order to truly find meaning in life and make it a worthy existence for everyone in our home environment. Keeping common courtesy, respect for one another and validating one another is a critical aspect to maintaining harmony in the home. We validate each other in the home by paying attention to each other's needs and caring for each other emotionally, mentally, physically and spiritually.

PEARL #12

Make The Home A Conflict–free Abode!

Dadashri – Are any arguments happening at all?

Questioner – There is no disturbance of peace at all in the home, so it is hard to really tell.

Dadashri – There are no differences of opinion with the husband or children at all?

Questioner – Well out of obligatory duty I have to quarrel with the children, nothing else much more than that.

Dadashri – There is no such thing as a duty to scold. How can it be that there is duty to quarrel with one's own children?!

Questioner – If they do not study, do their things, then of course we have to tell them.

Dadashri – Does the mother dog say anything to the puppy; does she need to say anything to the puppy? Despite this the puppies turn out alright, right!

Questioner – Is it because I believe that it has to be this way?

Dadashri – So you mean that it is in your belief to be enemies with your son? You believe it is okay to give pain to the poor boy?

Questioner – So this is why agitating loss of peace is experienced.

Dadashri – No, no. It's not like that, keep affection for him, and give him an affectionate hug. If a mother's real love is there, then children blossom, just like a rose blossoms they blossom like that. These children have all withered. What are withered children going to do?! So children blossom with the gentle caress of a mother's real love! Just a flower blossoms like that. Is love not needed, sister?

Questioner – Yes, it is needed.

Dadashri – So are you spanking them, flaring–up your chest?

Questioner – No, no, no, we are not doing that.

Dadashri – So, you are raising the children in a decent manner, all the focus and attention ought to get spent on this! So everyone in the home brims with bliss, harmony, and peace, everyone, our husband, and children stay in joy that is how it should be! Make the home like a garden. In that home over there, there is no synergy; the man will demand to know why the yogurt curry is made badly. Then the woman will yell back that the man is that way and this way. With fights, all these quarrels and arguments, how can it be called a home?! Rather, please forget about religious rituals even and focus on this first! Repair this situation first that needs dire attention then do your religious rituals. People have taught those religious rituals that are better off on the top shelf! First, repair the relational scars, wounds in the hearts and minds between the people in the home. There should not be any conflict in the home. Whomever's home there is no conflict, there stays the fragrance of the *Lord* and if even spontaneously by chance conflict slips in through the cracks, the *Lord* leaves.

Questioner – Religious rituals (*puja*) is done regularly every day.

Dadashri – It is not a question of religious rituals, but there should not be any conflict between the people in the home. In any given month, there should not be any clashing between people in the home on any day. If the religious rituals happen less, *that* is okay, The *Lord* is not starving for those religious rituals. The *Lord* only sees whether there is unity in the home or conflict! If there is conflict then He is not willing to stay around and if there is unity then He never wants to leave. What do you feel is beneficial?

Questioner – That if there is unity.

Dadashri – Yes, so create such clarity and purity in the home that under any circumstances, there is no conflict in the home. So, do not let conflict happen in the home, that is the first–and–foremost cultured inner living (*dharma*) and second comes spirituality for liberation (*moksha dharma*). That's it; there are only these two types of *dharma*. Will you fix the home? Hmmm?

Questioner – Yes, certainly we will fix it!

Dadashri – Yes..... Then let that be!

Insights From Pearl #12

'Charity begins at home,' as present Holistic Guide Kanudadashri affectionately told us. The first home is *within* oneself! When we have peace *within* ourselves, when we have found meaning in our lives from *within*, then only we can share that with others in our home environment, community, city, state, country and world at-large. It all begins with number one. Rituals are secondary to the importance of peace and harmony in the home of mind-speech-body. If rituals cause agitation and discord in the home, they are not necessary or can be done when there is quiet time and no one is disturbed by them.

PEARL #13

Live Life Without Distressful Conflict

The *Lord* does not go at all to certain people's places; but even where He does go when conflicts arise He will say, 'Let us get leave from this place, we are not comfortable here. We cannot bear it in this distress–filled noisy drama.' So, He instead goes to temples and churches. Then, there is conflict created in the churches. There is theft and lechery there; so He says, 'Let us leave from here now too'. Even the *Lord* is bored, sick-and-tired with all of this nonsense.

In our home we should be living a conflict–free life, so we should cultivate the art of knowing how to do so. If nothing else is known then we help those in the home understand that, if there is conflict the *Lord* will leave our home. Hence, you make a firm commitment that you do not want to engage in any conflicts and together you both decide that you do not want to engage in any conflict. After making the firm decision, if conflict arises, then know it happened outside of your sphere of power, so even if the husband is creating conflict you should cover yourself with a blanket and go to sleep. He, too, will go to sleep after a short while! And what if you had opposed him and started shouting back at him!?

Insights From Pearl #13

Just like anything else in life, when we make the firm commitment and conviction and conscious inner effort to live conflict-free in the home; the art of doing so will naturally reveal itself. The key is to understand how important it is to our *own* happiness and the happiness of our family. Once we fully understand the importance, the ways-and-means will come to us both from *within* and from *without*. We will attract what we need to accomplish our conviction. We hold within our hearts, wisdom, from infinite lives and when we learn to listen to and with the heart; the art of living will undoubtedly blossom.

PEARL #14

Wrongful Earning Will Cause Distressful Conflict

In Mumbai, I questioned a lady from a highly aristocratic family group, 'There is no conflict in home, right?' Then the lady says, 'Every morning there is a *breakfast of clashes* only!' I responded, 'Then, you surely save money on the cost of the breakfast, right?' The lady replied, 'No, still the betel leaves must be served, the betel leaves and spreading of butter on bread goes on *regardless*.' So, the conflicts and breakfast simultaneously go on! Poor fools, what kind of beings are you?

Questioner – In some homes the wealth must be of such a nature that causes conflicts to arise?

Dadashri – Only because of the nature of the wealth this happens. By rule, if the nature of wealth is honest and fair, then everything stays well balanced, the mind stays cool and calm. Dirty money has found its way into the home that is why conflicts happen. We decided from a young age that ill–earned money should not be allowed into the home, if by chance due to extraneous circumstances if it should get in, then leave it in the business; do not let it come into the home. Today sixty–six years have passed but ill–earned money has not been allowed to enter the home and neither has conflict ever arisen in the home. In the home it was decided that the home should be run with a certain amount of money. Even if the business earns hundreds of thousands of rupees, we decided that if this 'Patel' goes to work a job, how much salary would he get? At most, he would earn six hundred to seven hundred rupees. Business is just a swell from merit-filled karmas! Therefore, whatever would be earned in working, only that amount can be brought in the home, the rest should be left in the business. If a letter comes from the "income tax" office, we tell them, 'pay them from that reserve balance we have.' When which "attack" will come from what direction there is no telling and if the "attack" comes from the income tax office and that money has been spent up, then here on the spot we will have a heart "attack"! The "attacks" have permeated from every which direction, right? How can this be called a life? That perilous mistake we must break.

Insights From Pearl #14

This is amazingly brilliant thinking! The concept of living according to one's 'natural' income and not allowing 'dirty' money to come into the home is simply brilliant common sense. It keeps away negative influences and negative energy from entering the home. This way, the influences of the outside world in our home world are kept to a minimum; especially those influences that are not going to make the *quality* of our lives any better but rather bring quarrel, discontentment and misery not to mention perverse intellect. So, even if we own our own business or work at a job, we can figure-out how much we need to spend for our home and set that as a limit for our household. Any extra income can be kept as an emergency fund for unexpected things that may arise. So, peace of mind is never lost with this simple formula for commerce in living life which in today's world is more than half the battle of living peacefully!

PEARL #15

Just Give It A Trial Run

Just make a firm decision not to have conflict! Just make a decision to try it for three days! What is the harm in doing a trial? You fast for three days, right, for health reasons? Similarly, this, too; just try it. Everyone in the home comes together and decides that the discussion that Dada is having, we really liked it a lot. Then, let us break the vicious cycle of conflict from today! Then see what happens.

Insights From Pearl #15

Once we understand the importance of something, we surely will at least give it a trial run. If a trusted doctor recommends something to us, we try it because we trust the doctor. Similarly, if we want to accomplish something in our lives, and a trusted guide recommends it, why would we not try it?! Conflict begets more conflict whereas co-operation begets co-operation and peaceful co-existence.

It is incredibly freeing to have resolution and serenity within oneself and engaging in conflict with anyone does not truly accomplish this! What we see in others is just a reflection of what resides in us. The world is like a mirror that reflects back what is within us. We can actively work within ourselves to project what is virtuous and positive within us rather than the opposite. Where we put our focus is what magnifies in our lives. Why not put our focus on what is positive?!? It makes perfect logical sense to want to compound what is positive rather than negative if we think clearly about this reality of life.

PEARL #16

The Whole Day Long Is Passed In Distressful Conflicts

Questioner – But our people are such that until and unless there is an argument with the wife, life is just not any fun.

Dadashri – Yes, after the argument he has fun! Because a dog chews on a bone, now if we look at it if we wash the bone even a drop of blood does not come out; but the dog as it chews and presses harder and harder blood keeps flowing. Now, the blood is actually coming from the dogs own gums, but the dog thinks it is coming from the bone. This is how worldly life goes on!

The blind one spins a rope and the calf chews it up; that namely is worldly life. The blind one keeps spinning the rope trying to find the rope in front of him and the rope has fallen behind him while the calf is chewing on it. Similarly, all the activities of the ignorant go wasted and after dying the next life is ruined and human life is not even begotten! The blind one twining a rope erroneously believes, 'The rope has become 50 feet long.' And when he goes to get it wonders, 'What happened here?' Poor misguided one; the calf chewed it all up!

Insights From Pearl #16

Arguments never solve anything. If anything, they lead to more dissention and separation, which in turn, leads to escalated conflicts. When we disrespect, dishonor, or demean anyone, we are essentially doing so to ourselves especially when they are those with whom we share a place of inhabitance. We lower ourselves to below the level of a human being when we engage in behavior that is argumentative and falsely satisfy the crazy ego within that has no purpose but to destroy hearts and minds, especially our own. It is up to us to cherish, uphold and protect the hearts and minds of those closest to us. That is in our best and highest interest. It is a wild and crazy ego that enjoys purposely making conflict. That is not an ego that leads a human life but rather a barbaric life that does not contribute anything of value to oneself or others.

PEARL #17

The Disgraceful Pathetic Waste Of Infinite Energy

Like this, people keep earning money from a young age, but if they go to look in their "bank" account, there is only two thousand in the account. And all day long nothing but tension, tension, the whole day noisy drama, conflict and distressful escalated wrangles with others! Now, there is infinite energy *within* and what you think, project and visualize on the *inside* can manifest on the outside there is *that* much power *within*; but unfortunately forget thoughts on the *inside*, even what is attempted to be done grossly from the *outside* does not happen. Then tell me, what disgraceful, pitiable stunts have humans pulled!?

Insights From Pearl #17

Our priorities in life through lack of correct understanding have become skewed and distorted. People are more important than things! This basic truth has been lost in the quest for comfort, luxury and status. There is infinite energy within oneself that has been lost in this craziness. The human race is the one with the greatest power of all life forms. The power of choice lay *within* the human race. Why waste it away in useless petty conflicts and drama? The Holistic Master Guide' language sounds harsh, but it was out of His compassion and grace His words flowed. What *we* as humans project from *within* is what manifests in our world. Cultivating a positive inner attitude of gratitude coupled with cultivating inner virtues gives rise to tremendous inner strength and power to manifest positive outcomes in life.

PEARL #18

Distressful Conflicts Arise From Giving Pain

With giving rise to situations that give pain or suffering to others, we give rise to conflict within and with others.

And with the "wife" there can never be noisy drama. The one with whom you have to stay permanently in this life, there if you engage in noisy destructive drama together, then you both become happy, right, then tell me?

Questioner – No, it does not happen. Pain happens.

Dadashri – For both?

Questioner – Yes.

Dadashri – And in this case if one person does noisy *distasteful* drama then he alone is miserable *himself* only. In this whether the one listening suffers or not is up to them; to suffer is *only* due to one's own erroneous understanding *only*.

Questioner – If one does not want to engage in conflict and yet it still happens then who can gain victory over this?

Dadashri – Gold can gain victory! Will gold not gain victory? If gold is put on them, they become cool! Seriously speaking, to stay and stay together free of conflicts *that* namely is *living*. Conflicts should not arise. No one should get pain in the household. Every day, ask the husband, 'Tell me if there is anything that is hurting you.' Likewise he asks you as well.

Questioner – I ask every day.

Dadashri – What do you ask? That, if something is bothering you; just tell me, like that?

Questioner – Of course he does not ever tell anything! We make sure we do not let that kind of pain fall upon him.

Dadashri – In this, if the husband is a good one, he does not *give* pain. On the other hand, the children will give pain. Despite that they come from one's own womb, they give such pain that it *really* hurts the heart.

Insights From Pearl #18

Pain begets pain. Who likes pain? Most people do not want pain. They perhaps fall into a bad habit of being in a circle of pain due to lack of proper understanding and difficult circumstances. This vicious cycle must be broken if we are to keep our status as human beings! Our goal is to have inner peace, harmony and true affection in our homes. So, by having the correct understanding and learning to listen to each other's hearts, we can accomplish this. It is not rocket science. We must make it an anomaly that a dispute or conflict should ever arise in the home. The home is a haven where our hearts can be open and we can be ourselves. That is the true definition of a "*home*".

Using the simple platinum keys of "avoid clashes" and "adjust everywhere" from the heart center will surely aid in keeping conflicts out of our home. Furthermore, kind honesty is a good rule of thumb to keep in the home. If something needs to be said and it is not pleasant, many times, a kind silence does wonders without having to utter a single word! Empowering others with genuine encouragement and kindness can move mountains that seemed insurmountable from an intellectual perspective!

PEARL #19

Correct Understanding Heals Relative Relational Life

In reality, where is there even such a thing such as conflict in this world? Conflict means erred understanding! Wherever there is a lack of correct understanding there is conflict and wherever there is a lack of correct understanding there is pain and suffering. The pain and suffering, it is pain due to not finding correct understanding.

Questioner – Is it because of this conflict that a person's absorbed inner focus goes towards true dispassionate detachment (*vairagya*)?

Dadashri – The indifference that arises due to conflict with others, that indifference will further sink a person into the deepest darkest depths of relative worldly life; rather, if this indifference is avoided it is better. True dispassion (*vairagya*) should be according to perfect understanding. True dispassion with perfect understanding is extremely helpful. Otherwise, all these other forms or levels of indifference are useless. Why do people drink *'cyanide'*? Because they experience some form of indifference, right? When faiths in one's own self, one's own being *dies*, then that is when "poison" is sought, right? No farm animals lose faith or belief in their self. Besides the human race there is no other life form that loses faith in their self. It is only the human beings that are so incredibly vulnerable. Because they use their intellect they are vulnerable. They have been called unprotected, without shelter (*nirashriit*) by the *Lord*. All other life forms are directly protected by nature (*ashriit*). The protected have no fear. Crows and other birds all of them do they have any pain? Those that roam freely in the jungle, wild animals, all of them have no pain or suffering. Only those that have come into the close company of humans such as dogs, cats, cows, chickens have come to know suffering. Actually, humans are from the very core a suffering species; and whomever comes into close proximity to humans, lives in their company, all suffer with them (due to the inner enemies of anger, pride, deceit, greed, aversion and affinity of humans).

Insights From Pearl #19

Who can give us correct understanding? Only one who has it! So, when we surrender our ego at the divine lotus feet of a self-realized spiritual guide such as a Gyani Purush. Through His grace, we can acquire that correct understanding. Through that "correct understanding" relative relational life comes to a place of purity and normality that before was impure and abnormal due to the lack of correct understanding. True divine dispassion is something that is *'within'* and cannot be perceived by others and actually results in inner bliss not anguish and despair to the point of being suicidal. So, in order to be 'protected', we must take the shelter of a self-realized spiritual guide and live by the divine understanding that He bestows upon us. Then, our faith in ourselves can be properly restored and remain unshakeable from the core.

PEARL #20

Where Distressful Conflict Is Broken, There Is Delight

If conflict escalates then that is called 'disturbing interaction' (*kankaas*), really how can people want to be in friendship with those who have disturbing interactions?

Where there is sour buttermilk, if they go there to make it normal, instead their own becomes sour as well! From these sort of people it is ideal if a distance can be kept, or if you have become a *'Gyani'* it is fine. If he is a *'Gyani'* then he has full perfect understanding that the "record" sounds from all directions. The soul within is pure right! But they are trapped in this "jail'" then what can they do? What is the nature of this trap of distressing conflicts in the home? Everyone in the home gangs–up on ONE person in the household. And 'war' in the home *only*, what state of living results from this? If the friend asks him to come over and have dinner at the friend's house, he has to tell his friend no because there will be chaotic clashes at home. The poor guy does not even get to peacefully sleep at home! Every passing moment there is tension—filled conflict, and that, too, he has to, without a choice, suffer through it. What perplexing manifestations of past karmas, and that, too, one's own and only one's own! This world is such that it is impossible to be set free from feeling the intense heat of life's myriad experiences.

The best and primary step to freedom (*mukti*) is to break conflict PERIOD. To break conflict is reaching the pinnacle of the boundless bliss. Even if there is no eternal knowledge (*gyan*) but that there is relative karmic responsibility, when can it be said? Well, no matter what kind of environment, difficult circumstances are faced in the home, they are quietly endured; and even in clash—filled situations one does not give rise to conflict with others, does not create an inferno of fire! That itself alone is called 'nobility'!! Until then, the *Lord's* fragrance will persist in the home. In the home where there is conflict with one another, everything is going to be destroyed. The *Lord's* fragrance most definitely is lost but even wealth walks out the door.

A home focused on humane heart-centered inner living (*dharmishta*) will not allow conflicts to arise and by chance, if on some blue moon, it happens; then the doors are closed and it is properly resolved within the closed doors of the home and a keen vigilance is kept that this type of conflict should not arise again.

Insights From Pearl #20

The Holistic Master Guide's simple prescription of "avoid clashes" and "adjust everywhere" when applied to everyday life in a practical manner will infuse an aura of peace, tranquility and bliss that cannot be broken even by the most vicious of circumstances. The decision must be made by oneself! It is for the sake of preserving one's *own* inner peace and bliss. If it is done with correct understanding, the inner peace and serenity will certainly manifest and prevail even without self-realization.

The ego must be softened with the understanding of what makes life meaningful and actually gives us peace and happiness. Finding faults in others, especially, in the home makes for a miserable existence and breakdown of the family altogether! What is our life for anyways? To waste away in negativity? It is up to us to make the firm commitment and decision to maximize this gift of human life and do the introspective work *within* to make that happen.

True affection does not even require words. It is something that is conveyed by the heart center to those who reside there. Those who benefit from the compassion that flows from there sometimes do not even know it! That is the beauty of it all.

PEARL #21

There Is Bliss Where The Mind Is Free From Conflict

The *Lord* asks, 'Till when is there worldly life (*sansar*)?' Well He replies, 'As long as there is a mind occupied with conflict.' If the mind becomes clear without any conflict, there is blissful freedom from within (*mukti*), thereafter no matter where the mind travels serenity persists.

This little boy who listens to our speech, too, feels coolness within, he, too, can understand the difference, and distinguish, between cool water and boiling water. When there is a quarrel at home, then he comprehends the situation as "pappa" told "mummy" this and "mummy" told "pappa" that. And furthermore, he draws the conclusion within him that, 'That one seems to be crooked. And I am just a kid so right now I have no power to do anything, but when I get older it will be payback time.' The little boy can decipher the difference between conflict–filled eyes and cool compassionate eyes.

Insights From Pearl #21

Clarity is something we all seek in our lives. It is such an amazing feeling when the mind & heart are in unison. When we find that clarity *within* ourselves, it will emanate outwards to our family members and the world at-large. What we put-out and give-out to our loved ones is what we will get back. If we mistreat those under our care, we will surely have to face the consequences. The mind gets serene and content with the correct understanding. So, it behooves us to understand ourselves, what is in our best interest and what is not and this way the mind will not be at odds with our hearts once the understanding is correct and clear.

PEARL #22

Living Driven By Distressful Conflicts

Even in these mansions bliss was not found! Such huge mansions!! Look at how much light there is in these mansions, red, green lights, stacks of stainless steel plates, but yet blissful joy was not found. All day long spinning around in a confused stupor...! These crows, sparrows all see the platforms and sit together in unity and these people never sit together in unity! Right now they are probably sitting at the table quarreling, because that type is not straightforward and simple from the very beginning. They were not simple and straight forward in times when life was not so complex and sophisticated; then what can be expected in this complex age of clash and conflict?! This type itself is egotistical right! All these cows and bulls are "regular"; they do not make any confusion, because they are all naturally protected (*ashriit*). Only humans are unprotected (*nirashriit*) that is why all humans worry. Otherwise, in the whole world no animals or even *demi–gods* or *angels* engage in futile worry.

So, only humans are going to worry. Despite living in such beautiful mansions they carry around limitless apprehensions! Right now while sitting down to eat they are thinking about the shop that the gate was left open, that person's rent is due! While sitting here eating he is immersed in worry and anxiety as though he was not going to go there right now?! Oh why do you not let it be! Just eat at least in peace!! But he does not even eat in a proper manner. He remains agitated from inside because the gate was left open. Then because he is agitated, he uses it as an excuse to start a quarrel with the wife. Poor fool, why do you take out your frustration on someone else or your wife for that matter?! That is why our *Kaviraj* has sung, 'The inferior husband oppresses the wife.' Where else can he get away with being dictatorial? If he goes out to do it to someone else, he will get beaten! So, tyrannical at home!! Is this becoming of us? Does it make us look good? Within each and every one of us there is incredible power! In this, it is not his fault either. The knowledge that he or she has gotten, is backwards, that is why he walks backwards. If he gets the forward-facing correct knowledge, then he is such that he will walk in that direction. After you received the correct elevating knowledge, your inner power and strength has multiplied so dramatically! Intuitive forward vision has compounded tremendously!!

Insights From Pearl #22

Only when we experience the negative impact that distressful conflicts are having in our lives, we will truly understand how much damage distressful conflicts cause in our lives. The key is awareness and the commitment to "avoid conflicts" and "adjust everywhere" as the Divine Holistic Master Guide has simply put in straightforward language. How we treat our closest family members is a reflection of how we value our own selves.

As Holistic Guide Kanudadashri has said, "Charity begins at home." When we respect, honor, validate ourselves as human beings, we are able to do the same for others. Virtues such as humility, kindness, simplicity, honesty, flexibility, generosity, and sweetness begin to blossom from within. When we treat our family members with disrespect, disregard, contempt and dishonor; in actuality, we are hurting ourselves as much if not more. It wears away at our own self-esteem when we cannot see the virtues and divinity in those who reside with us.

What good are luxuries without those whom we hold in our hearts? Comfort and luxury make us apathetic and numb to what matters most in life which are the human beings in our lives. It is all about prioritizing in the correct order. If we value things, fame and fortune more than our loved ones, they, too, will learn the same. Setting appropriate priorities in life becomes a driving force in finding meaning, contentment, peace and harmony in life.

PEARL #23

Conflicts Invade From Every Which Direction

Do you think that there is only one type of squash? How many kinds of squash are there? Each and every head (mind) has a different perspective! And until when could it still be called a head (mind)? Well, until it does not let conflict ooze into the home and there was that much diligence. Only then they could truly be called heads (mind)! Today, they let conflict enter the home so they are *gullible*, thus called pumpkins! At this time have conflicts permeated the home or not? Even if the husband does his hair a certain way, they creep in do they not? In the end if nothing else, conflicts creep in with some random gossip or news. The doors are kept locked, there is even a top lock and chain so the door is only opened if the bell rings; despite these extreme measures with some random gossip or news conflicts still find their way into the home. Why do we call them pumpkins? Because despite eating their own home's food, wearing their own home's clothes and no one out there is stealing yet still they engage in distressful conflicts with each other. Even though it is made in the home and used in the home as well; this is how (ridiculous) people have become!

Insights From Pearl #23

Our intellects should be cultivated in such a manner that it brings us peace, serenity and contentment in living our lives in a meaningful manner. This cannot be accomplished by watching the world and what the world is displaying to us outwardly. We must learn to view our own world *within*. The only way to accomplish this is through introspection. We must learn to know our own mind, our own intellect, our own heart, our own ego, our own reflective consciousness which namely is our world! Where are we going wrong that we cannot even enjoy our own hard-earned money in our own home? We cannot allow the sound bites, standards and styles of the world to dictate our world to a point of bringing us distress. That is ludicrous! No one lives our lives but us! Why vicariously live through others? Especially, if that brings us pain and suffering? There is so much noise in the world, we must develop selective hearing to listen to that which is beneficial to us and will bring us greater satisfaction and meaning in living our lives. The goal is to be the best human beings that we can possibly be! It is ideal if we are giving more through our positivity than we are taking from this world! This way, we are leaving an earth that is better for our future generations to come. After all, it is collectively our earth as the human race!

PEARL #24

Relative Living Ought To Be Without Conflict

The whole world is frenzied in meticulous attention to multiply, *gather*. There is no need to be fastidiously careful as there is no need to be nonchalantly careless either! It is not necessary to be over–careful in multiplying or gathering nor is it necessary to carelessly deplete either. In this it is that all day long is spent in painstaking attention, meticulous care and more finicky precaution! Even so, nothing is being spilled and there are no difficulties arising either! So much eating and drinking is transpiring, there is so much being earned yet no one is happy? How ironic is this?! In relative life there should at least be no distressful conflict right? Is relative life meant to be conflict–filled? Relative living is in itself by its nature conflict–free. Only, how to live relative relational life is not known, that is why conflicts arise with others.

Insights From Pearl #24

Excess is poison! Greed of all sorts has resulted in us living our lives blindly without purpose, meaning or satisfaction. What good is accumulating that leads to anxiety, distress and suffering? The true art of living must be sought out! Less is more in today's complex world of too much of everything. Choices, choices and more choices lead to fickle, shallow and short attention spans. When our focus turns *inward* to cultivating our inner virtues, the attention becomes steady and introspection allows for clarity of thought.

Truly Cultured Living Is Where Conflict Is Diminishing

There is so much worry and restless tension! No differences are being dissolved, even so in the mind one believes that so much spiritual good has been done! Poor fool, have you managed to solve differences at home? Have they even become less? Do you worry less? Has some peace been gained? Then, the poor fool will say, 'No, but I have done so much spiritual good, have I not?' Misguided one, what heart-centered inner living (*dharma*) did you accomplish? True inner cultured living gives peace inside; mental anguish, physical illness and stressful reactions (*adhi–vyadhi–oopadhi*) do not happen, that is namely relative inner cultured living! To go towards one's real essence of being, that can be called heart-centered inner cultured living. Rather the resulting conflict–ridden manifestations in daily life go on increasing!

All these paths exist and backward paths exist *too*, but the "highway" is altogether a different matter. There is a lot of side and back streets besides the 'highway'. Within the path of the "highway", in the home despite there being everyone, the wife, the children, conflicts do not happen; then we can be sure we are on the "highway"; if not we are on some side road going who knows where! There are so many different roads. There should be some "level" way to know them right! In which case, we should surely stay on the "highway". Dear lady, are you able to tell, figure–out whether there is conflict or if there is not?

Questioner – Yes, it can be figured–out.

Dadashri – That is all that must be vigilantly overseen and if there are no conflicts happening in the home then know that we are surely on the right path. The path of liberation (*mukti*) is *different* and heart-centered inner living is *different*. Worldly religions for spiritual living are correct, but there should not be any conflicts in the home. And if there is conflict and still to *insist* that our religious path is still correct then that is *dogmatism*. They only defend their *dogmatism* about the religion. They are not protecting their souls. So, when conflicts in the home subside, then we can be convinced that we may have gained some wisdom of inner cultured living. *Dogmatism* is uselessly going around carrying a heavy load in the mind, that I *do* something important. I am of *this* religion, and of this particular religious sect. Oh pathetic zombie, there are excessive amounts of conflicts in the home.

Your face looks like you just drank castor oil all the time. Where there is heart-centered inner living, do the faces look like they just drank castor oil? There is *biting* from within. It is because the true meaning of heart-centered inner cultured living has not been understood, *that* is why!

If heart-centered inner cultured humane living (*dharma*) and conflicts are really flowing simultaneously then the conflicts should be on the decline. If conflicts are diminishing then know that the heart-centered inner cultured humane living (*dharma*) is doing its job, but what if conflicts just are not being reduced at all, then what? And wherever, whenever conflicts arise undoubtedly there is absence of heart-centered inner humane living (*adharma*) only. "COMPLETE" absence of heart-centered inner humane living (*adharma*), in the name of religious living there is a perpetual absence of heart-centered inner humane living (*adharma*) only. Despite this, the world still goes on like this right!

Insights From Pearl #25

Harmony, peace and affection in our homes is far more valuable and important that any rituals or religious practices. If the belief system that one has adopted into one's life is not bringing peace, harmony and joy in our homes, of what use is it? 'Home' means starting with oneself only! If we, ourselves, are not at peace, then of what value is our faith in any religion or religious practice? Our understanding is definitely *erred* at some point. The religion is not at fault. Our own perception and understanding is *erred*. So, it behooves us, as the stars of our own lives, to gain the correct understanding that will enable us to live peacefully, harmoniously and contentedly. An excellent gage for going to an introspective mode is whether conflicts are on the rise or decline, especially in our immediate personal lives with those closest to us.

PEARL #26

Dada Shows Such A Way Of Heart-Centered Inner Living

People only need to be shown a way of heart-centered inner living (*dharma*) so that conflicts do not happen in their homes, a conflict–filled life does not remain at all. At this time heart-centered inner living (*dharma*) has become "upset". So these people are living conflict–ridden lives, if not are these people of different religions guilty of something? It is not like that, regardless why there is so much worry and anxiety?! Well, because the whole life itself is full of nothing but conflicts *within* that manifest on the *outside* with others.

All religions were originally designed to create peace and harmony in the home that at this time have turned upside–down. So what is turned upside–down, we will turn upside-down again to return it all to an upright position. A life without conflicts can happen so spontaneously and naturally in actuality! And we will give a way of inner cultured living that is effortless to these people. What effort can we expect from people whose faces look like they just drank castor oil all the time?! Do people not look like castor oil faces out there? Would they really be purposely putting castor oil on their faces and go around everywhere? Why would they? It is not smart to give these people the trouble of effort, it is unwise to make them do penance–renunciation (*taap–tyaga*), they are already miserable. Again they will be told to give up eating certain things. Why ask him to stop eating that when that is all the poor guy likes to eat? It is not wise to ask the guy to give up things or renounce things (*tyaga*). He does not have any kind of joy whatsoever to begin with! Compassion overflows in us is such the state of things! We see all this through our *intuitive* inner vision, so we overflow with compassion that from this; *this* miserable suffering people must be freed.

Insights From Pearl #26

The Holistic Master Guide overflowed with compassion as He saw the miserable, pitiful state of the people of this turmoil-filled age of clash and conflict. He had a deep inner intent in His heart center to give people something that would *free* them from this state of misery. There are so many tools He has left us with such as the Obstruction Removing *Tri-Mantra, Namaskar Vidhi, Naav Kalamo, Kaviraj Paado, Kirtan Bhakti* to help us achieve some inner peace and positive, balanced intellect. Not everyone is necessarily seeking absolute liberation, but surely all people desire to live a happy, balanced, meaningful life. He understood with His holistic inner vision that to ask people to renounce anything would be asking too much in an age when most people barely make it through the day as it is! So, in all His grace, He gave alternative tools that do not require any such renunciation of anything of that sort. Depending on the personality type, there are enough tools in the treasure chest to fit all personality types! So, even if someone has not become self-realized by being initiated with the self-realization ceremony, there are enough alternative tools such as *Tri-Mantra, Kirtan Bhakti* and *Naav Kalamo* for people of all walks of life to gain the inner life understanding to help manifest inner peace, serenity, healing and empowerment in living their daily lives.

Perverse Intellect Fuels Distressful Conflicts

Where there is disturbing loud interaction, where there is conflict, that home is not inviting to anyone and really there is no valid reason for the disturbing loud interactions at all. Especially in cultured households there really is no reason for it whatsoever, but what can people do if their understanding is erroneous? Due to madness they just keep having loud disturbing interactions with others.

Questioner – Is it because some people just have in the nature of their personality to be loud and have disturbing conflicts with others?

Dadashri – That is precisely why I am saying that there is not any pain but it is given fuel to arise, it is being "invited". No one *really* has any pain of any sort. There is plenty of food of all sorts, clothing and accessories to wear, shelter is free and clear, everything that is needed is there, but pain is being fueled to arise. There are a very small percentage of simple, straightforward people. Otherwise, it is all "rubbish material". "Rubbish" yet intellectually sharp, talented these people are. The intellect which is there, it is *perverse* intellect; the small part of the intellect that is developed, it is possible to turn it around to be positive and uplifting. If close "touch" is met with us then it can be transformed. Humane inner culture and proper guidance is needed. It is not a totally lost cause. There is not a total lifeless, inanimate state in people. Not only useless, false intellect but even out right *rotten* intellect has arisen. Before, it was not even rotten. If intellect has gone bad, then it has potential to be reformed. Only because the intellect has at least been "developed", that is why it is possible

Lord Krishna has said that there are two types of intellect, positively balanced (*avybhichairini*) intellect and perverse (*vybhichairini*) intellect. Perverse intellect means it only generates pain and suffering within oneself and positively balanced intellect means it only generates contentment and bliss within. The positively balanced intellect discovers the bliss in the pain and suffering, those with positively balanced intellect will even eat basmati rice with dirt in it without being agitated from within or complaining about it. Here, in America, the food is so delightful, you get clean *ghee*, you get yogurt ready–made. Such delightful food! Life is simple and straightforward, despite this the art of living is not known; thus, that is why the inner beatings are taking place.

At least what is in our best interest should be questioned and thoughtfully researched! Is it in our best interest to preserve and live our lives with the delight and contentment we had when we got married; or the "shock" that we experienced on the day we became widowed?! It is to our advantage and in our best interest to keep the delight and contentment of the day that we got married. What good is the "shock" of the day we got widowed to us? When two people sit together to get married; surely one will be left alone without exception. This comes with the contract to every marriage so what is there to get into loud disturbing conflicts about? Where the terms of the contract are already decided, then it is out of the question to even think about disturbing conflicts. Does not one of the two have to be widowed at some point or not?

Insights From Pearl #27

What is a distinctive virtue of all those who have attained praiseworthy things in their lives? A common golden thread is a positive inner attitude of gratitude and giving from within. There is no obstacle, barrier, adversity, turmoil or challenge that a positive attitude will not carry one through with minimal collateral damage. Furthermore, pearls of wisdom of experience are gathered at every turn with a positive inner attitude. A positive attitude from within can only result when the intellect is positively balanced. A person with an inner positive attitude can make lemonade from lemons at every turn in their life. And it seems like that person has no problems! In actuality, it is that inner attitude that keeps them breezing through all of life's trials, tribulations, adversity and obstacles. The sooner we start counting the blessings and blessing the curses in our lives the more meaningful and amazing our lives will undoubtedly become for ourselves and for others who come into contact with us.

PEARL #28

Our Thoughts At The Time Of Marriage

We had the realistic awareness while we were in the marriage ceremony itself! We were aware that we were tying ourselves to a new life partner. We are considered sons from the *Kshaitriya* Warrior class, in those days we wore prince–like turbans and all dressed–up at the age of 15–16 years looked so attractive brimming with an aura of virility and proud confidence. In those days, there was such incredible confidence and pride at that age, today it has all dried up, just like quash gets all shriveled–up. So, at the age of fifteen, we sat down to get married and did it with great celebratory style too! We took dowry, at that time we took three thousand rupees for dowry. We got married in the year 1923. Those were the times of serious economic depression; we had little money but still had a chariot with four horses with the procession and lit with flaming lamps. The lamps were lit with white lime.

Then I went to sit to get married in the decorated marriage gazebo. Shortly thereafter they delivered my bride, *Hiraba*, there across from me in the gazebo. Her maternal uncle walked her as a virgin bride; she was thirteen years old at the time. They had tucked a big thing of flowers on my turban, what is it called again? Oh yes, it's called a boutonniere. It had been put up there, and it came down like this over my eyes. So, *Hiraba* could not be seen. But, because I could not see her, I kept moving it around until... I saw her, then the thought came to me that wow, she is stunningly beautiful and I had seen her from childhood. My intentions her mother and father figured out. One time I had seen her in public. So, because people like to gossip, we did not say anything to each other but it was understood between us. Her family respected the fact that I kept her honor and understood how important her honor is. So, their daughter got taken.

Then finally the boutonnière moved and I thought within myself that although I am sitting down here to get married, she is truly amazing, but one of the two will surely be widowed at some point!

Questioner – At that tender age you had those thoughts?

Dadashri – Yes, darn it all, why would I not have them? One of the darn wheels of the chariot surely has to break at some point, right? A union initiated will not stay without termination at some point.

Questioner – But, at the time of marriage when that union was taking place, there is so much illusion of infatuation (*moha*), then how could You have such deep thoughts of true dispassionate detachment (*vairagya*)? But, darn it, at that time You had the thought of union and then the widow–ship that follows! One of the two will have to move on alone, either me or her!

Questioner 2 – So, did you feel the blissful joy of getting married after that?

Dadashri – There was never any blissful joy. It was only egotistical pride. Only that I thought that I am really something else, it was that joy. Our mother–in–law just kept looking at me repeatedly. That lady had charmed me (had me wrapped around her finger) at the age of fifteen, tucked at her waist. Oh, we could never find a son–in–law like this she would say. She even said that I had a round–round face like an Indian sweet ball (*ladoo*). So, she was in her illusory infatuation (*moha*) and me in my egotistical pride (*ahamkar*), but one wheel will surely break, there will surely be a widower at some point. Then what can we do about it?

When we go to marry people give us dowry. Who do they give it for? So that you can take the "wife" home and tie her up and beat her? Is that why they give dowry? Back in the day you know why they gave dowry, because they knew the household to be without any loud disturbing interactions! There is no loud conflicts, they do not give pain to each other, that should be the case *right*!?

Insights From Pearl #28

This amazing account of His own experience at the time of marriage is extremely telling of His elevated spiritually developed inner state at even such a young age. He knew Himself enough to be aware of His own weaknesses and the source of them as well. He was fully aware that anything in the worldly life is not forever. He understood the temporary nature of the sacred union of marriage. He was perfectly aware of His ego and the grip that the adoration of His mother-in-law to be had on Him as well. Furthermore, He knew why they agreed to give their daughter to His home as well. This was all at the young, tender age of 15. It truly speaks volumes of His elevated inner spiritual development before enlightenment took place at the age of 50 in 1958 in *Surat* in the state of Gujarat in India at the train station in the midst of a crowd.

PEARL #29

Extreme Measures To Rise Above Conflicts

Some people are from the very root with the innate relative nature of engaging in conflicts! But many people are so smart that they will go and fight outside but will not quarrel with the wife in the home. Believe it or not, there are so people that will even push their wives on the swing in the home! We had a contracting business so we even had to go to the homes of many people on business calls, we even drank their tea! We never have a sense of being separate from anyone. One day when I went over to a person's house, the man started pushing his wife on the swing! So, I asked him, 'Why do you do this, doesn't she try to dominate you then? Then, he replied, 'How is she going to dominate? She is helpless, she does not have anything.' Then I told him, 'Many husbands in our community are afraid if the wife gets dominating, then what will happen. So, we do not push them on the swing.'

Then, the wise man said, 'Do you know why we swing our wives? I only have two places to lay my head down. We do not have a bungalow. We only have two places to sleep and if there is quarreling with the wife, then where am I going to sleep? Then, my whole night will be ruined. So, instead I fight with people outside everywhere, but I keep it "clear" with the wife.' The wife will ask him, 'Why did you not bring the *pakoda* (an edible fried food) I asked you to bring this morning? He will give a sincere whole–hearted reply, 'I will bring it tomorrow.' And in the morning he will say again, 'I will bring it for sure today from wherever I have to.' Then, in the evening when he comes empty handed, the wife gets really stressed–out, but the man is so smart, he says, 'Ohhh…only I know my state of suffering!' So, he wins over the wife and makes her feel needed and special, he does not argue with her at all. And what do our community people say? 'What, are you nagging and pressuring me? Forget it; I am not going to get it.' Silly fool, this cannot be said to her, instead you break your weight with her (she loses respect for you). Since, it is you saying this; it is *you* who is actually repressed by her. Fool, how is she repressing you? When she speaks stay quiet. But with those that are very weak, easily agitated then when they get agitated we should just keep our mouths shut and listen to the 'record' play.

Whatever home does not have any quarrels is the greatest, *heck*, even if there are quarrels, but if there is a turn–around and resolution is made, even that is called great! The wise man even on a single day in the matters of food will not 'test' the wife if the man gets irritated and says, 'You are this or you are that' and if the wife gets agitated then he shuts up and immediately recognizes this will result in a fire! Therefore, we should be in our place and let her be in hers!!

People of each religious group have different customs and traditions. And each and every home has its own code of behavior, as each any every kitchen has its own way of running! Each "viewpoint" is different and distinctive; there is no way to align them, however, if there is no quarreling *that* is best.

Insights From Pearl #29

The Master Holistic Guide paints quite a picture here of an incident that left Him with pearls of wisdom about life and living as a business man who visited the homes of people of varied backgrounds. His observations were always geared at finding out what was working in society and what was not working at the home level to maintain peace and harmony. Even prior to attaining self-realization in 1958, from within, He was always in a mode of inner observation to understand optimizing human life and researching human behavior.

PEARL #30

Gentle Carefulness At The Time Of Conflicts

Because the conflict–generating intentions have disappeared from within us the people on the outside will not have any conflict–generating intentions either. Since, we do not get agitated, they, too cool down from within. Just become like a solid wall so nothing can be heard. It has been fifty years for us in marriage, but there has never been a difference of opinion between us on any single day. Even if she, *Hiraba*, is dripping *ghee* in front of my eyes I just quietly keep observing without a single word. We had awareness of inner understanding and knowledge at those times that she would never purposely spill *ghee*. Even if I tell her to do it, she would not do it. Would anyone purposely spill *ghee*? No. Even so, *ghee* spills that is something to be seen, so we just observe! Before any difference of opinion ever arises knowledge stays present *"on–the–moment"*.

The wise man's wife gets delighted and softened just as he confesses, 'Only I know what a terrible state I am in.' And many people do not talk of their feelings or anything like that. Poor fool, you are genuine if you share your pitiful state, tell her, 'It is just not possible, so please stay happy with me and support me.'

In everyone's presence, with the Sun God (*Surya Narayan Dev)* as a witness, with the Priest as a witness, the marriage contract was drawn, 'To stand firm with gentle carefulness through all times' (*samay varte savdhaan*). So, you do not know how to be 'gently careful' gentleman with her? According to the times of your lives, through the happenings of life, you should be a careful gentleman. So, the Priest chants, '*Samay varte savdhaan*... Through all times flowing with gentle carefulness.' So, the priest understands well enough, but what does the groom understand?! What is the meaning of '*savdhaa*'? Well, the Priest will say, 'When the bride gets fired-up with anger, then you become cool like spring water, be a gentleman.' So, '*samay varte savdhaan*', whatever times you face together, it is crucial that you remain with gentle care, only then can this journey of union in marriage be embarked upon in the worldly life. In this, if she is boiling in anger and we boil too, then that is not having gentle carefulness as a husband. When she boils we must cool ourselves *way* down. So, we stayed this way '*saavdha*' with *Hiraba*. We would never let the cracks and ravines form between us. As soon as a crack forms, we immediately "set" the "welding" process in motion.

But, if there is too much salt in the lentil curry, today they just let loose on everyone in the household; they do not think they should "adjust" themselves. So, the gist of the matter is that today there happens to be too much salt in the lentil curry; so a time has come for us to act with gentle care, maybe just eat a little less that day but do not make a big *rant* out of it. So, roll with the times as a careful gentleman. That is why I keep saying that you are not acting according to the demands of the times! You just lash out immediately in reaction. Oh pitiful zombie, even a young child can tell that it is too salty. Can they not? And this fool just blurts it out first without thinking at all!

Then the agitated wife will retaliate, 'I am not bringing you your plate, you come yourself. Now, your health has improved and you are mobile. You go out and socialize with people, go out here–and–there, smoke cigarettes and when it is dinner time, you have the nerve to ask for your plate?! I am NOT coming!' Then, we should quietly say, 'Please set the plate down there I am coming. It is my mistake here.' If we do this then the night will pass well, if not the whole night is ruined. The man who threw in the towel with his mistake has peacefully gone to sleep, while the woman who is still fuming and agitated cannot sleep. So, the next morning it drags on, will she not again rowdily slap down the tea cup and saucer in agitation? So, this man immediately understands that she is still upset! This is a life filled with conflicts.

Insights From Pearl #30

The highly developed social and interpersonal skills of the Holistic Master Guide are difficult to come by in today's confused, chaotic world. He never allowed a dispute to ever arise between Him and *Hiraba*. There would always be gentle carefulness at delicate times. He would never engage in the game of complaining about anything for over fifty years! He definitely had a treasure chest of riches residing within Him in the art of living life. He married at the age of 15 and *Hiraba* was only 13 years old. Yes, this was in a different time and age in the 1920s. That is the reality. However, the basic wisdom of the art of living is *timeless*. If we can make it a priority over everything else to be kind, loving and caring in the home, then that becomes the standard in the home. It is up to us to set the standard with *our* behavior. The positive power of one person's *positivity* in the home cannot be understated. Just as the negative impact of one's person's negativity can serve to wreck a home. So, as human beings who truly want to live the best possible life, it behooves us to utilize the master key of "gentle carefulness" or "*saavdhan*" when delicate situations arise in our home environment and life in general.

PEARL #31

You Cannot Become Peaceful By Bullying

Questioner – The main thing is that it should be so there is peace in the home.

Dadashri – But how can peace be kept? Even if the daughter is named "*Shanti*", peace does not stay. For this correct understanding of heart-centered inner living is needed. Everyone in the home should be told that, look, all of us in this house are not enemies, no one is out to pick fights, and there is no need for us to have dividing differences. Share the food with each other and eat together peacefully. No matter what there should not be loud verbal disturbing interactions with anyone in the household. What is the point of noisy conflicts with those under the same roof? It can never be that by bullying someone else that inner bliss will ever be experienced. And we give delight in order to get delight in return.

Only if we give joy in the home to others will we get it in return. Besides, only then will breakfast be made and served nicely and properly or else it will be served badly and made badly as well.

Insights From Pearl #31

Typically a bully does so out of a lack of personal self-esteem. If we are in a positive, balanced, serene state with ourselves; that aura will project effortlessly from within to others. So, the key is to begin with oneself. If we find ourselves behaving badly with someone close to us, we must necessarily step back and go *inward* to resolve the turmoil within that is causing this behavior. Perhaps, there is pent-up resentment, lack of forgiveness, lack of empathy, a difficulty in overcoming past events or whatever may be causing this unhealthy behavior. Once we discover where the problem resides, then we can apply the appropriate medication. The Holistic Master Guide has given us all the tools to utilize as needed, we must use our common sense to apply them appropriately or ask a trusted holistic inner science guide for assistance!

Is It Worth Creating Conflicts To Cover–Up Your So-Called Reputation?

First the guy will have gotten into a verbal spitting match with someone as he is walking outside or the boss chewed him out at work earlier that day so he comes home and starts yelling. Dear pathetic one, the delicious food that has been prepared; eat that first then open your mouth to speak. But no, first he has to kick his leg up poor zombie. He, the zombie, is crooked only *right*!? Have you or have you not ever seen someone like this at any place?

Questioner – That has been seen, I have seen them everywhere, I have even seen it in myself, the pots are only banging and clanging at everyone's place right!?

Dadashri – This really bores me to tears darn it, that in life there is all this eating–drinking beverages and what in the world is this? After eating home–made, hard-earned food to have bickering in the home?

One time, while our big brother's wife, our sister–in–law (*bhabhi*) had gone to start–up the stove, some guest arrived. For some odd reason our big brother was in a rush, so he pushed her to make tea quickly. But, *bhabhi* was putting a pin to get the stove going but it was not functioning properly. She was trying everything, blowing on it, tweaking it but it just was not working. This is a story of what happened some 60 years ago. So, what did our big brother do after this? He got mad and threw everything outside, in a flash! A burning stove he threw out with the teacups and saucers too he threw outside. All the guests were sitting in the front living room area. So, I questioned him, 'What will you do now?' So he panicked, 'What are we going to do about the *chai* now? Go and get *chai* from the backdoor from a restaurant or wherever.' I told him, 'I will not get *chai* from a restaurant here; I will get the neighbor's stove instead.' But, he broke the tea cups and saucers; it would still have been fine if he did not do it! What good did it do him? And, *bhabhi*, what could she do? If the stove went bad, what could she do?

Questioner – But, he did not understand that, right!

Dadashri – No, but what kind of guests are even bigger than the *Lord*?! We can just simply tell the guests, 'The stove is not starting up. Whoever is smart, can you get it started for us? We could simply just say that dear friend, just set it up for us! We had the right intentions to make *chai* for them. So, just because our reputation would get tarnished, so what for that create conflicts in the home?

This kind of lunacy is anyone ever able to forget (erase from the psyche)?! All of these kinds of senseless dramas have been witnessed right!

Questioner – Yes, they have.

Dadashri – So the burning stove has been seen splattered outside and the broken cups and saucers have been seen too!

Questioner – Many times all the frustration gets released by throwing. (It can be therapeutic.)

Dadashri – Well, by throwing the stuff out the turmoil did not go. Instead, *bhabhi* told me to go outside and get the cups even though big brother said not to! So, we had to get the cups and saucers and bring them back into the house. And the stove was fixed and brought back in the home to be used again! Well, did stoves come cheap back then?! It was seven rupees back then in the 1920s for an iron stove.

Questioner – Back in those days even seven rupees were not easy to come by.

Dadashri – Yes.

Insights From Pearl #32

Through His reflective inner vision, He re-told the story as He saw it 60 years ago! This experience at such a young age as a teen age boy, taught Him so much. He was able to deduce such pearls of wisdom at such a young age. He did not feel it was worth it to cause the people in the home turmoil and anguish just for the sake of so-called "reputation". What is 'real' reputation? 'Real' reputation is that if someone walks into our home they feel the aura of peace, serenity, wisdom, true affection and compassion. They *feel* it in their heart centers. We must create a "*home sweet home*" by letting peace begin with us. People are not stupid; they can make-out everything without being told. People can make-out whether our hospitality is genuine and natural or made-up for some ulterior motive. People appreciate honesty and genuine banter far more than trying to impress people with false pretenses of ego. Everyone has a heart center and intuitive sense *within* them and can sense our intentions. Instead, if we keep an open heart and open mind with all those who come to our home and business, they will go away with something that cannot have a price tag put on it. They will go away with satisfaction in their hearts of being treated genuinely with authenticity and *humanity*.

PEARL #33

Throw Out The Conflicts

Now, each and everyone does not want to have conflicts, but cannot help themselves. What can we do about it?

Nobody wants to have conflicts, right? But, the conflicts just happen, so what can be done? Do you understand conflicts? Do you live alone or with the family?

Questioner – Brother–sister, mother–father, I live with everyone.

Dadashri – In the home environment, there are days when conflicts just arise right?

Questioner – Sometimes they happen.

Dadashri – So, who throws out that disturbing force? Does it stay around all night long or do you throw it out?

Questioner – We throw it out.

Dadashri – How do you throw it out? Do you hit it with a wood cane? These people all want to throw out the conflicts, but how can they do it?

Questioner – (We do it by) by forgetting the conflicts and creating an atmosphere of joyful harmony in the home.

Dadashri – So, it is like this, all these "lives" have been "fractured", "minds" have been "fractured", intellects have been "fractured", what else can someone find in times like that? So, again the "minds" need to become *strong*. When can the "mind" become strong? When the *Gyani Purush* or Holistic Guide is seen live, just from seeing Him the "mind" gets stronger.

Insights From Pearl #33

As we observe, we learn. So, it is important to choose our mentors and guides wisely. When we observe the Holistic Master Guide, we can comprehend how He does not allow conflicts to arise. We can ask questions; get answers about life from those who have proven to overcome conflicts in their lives. We can ask our parents how they dealt with difficult situations in their lives to get direction. The key is to understand how much damage and how detrimental conflicts are to our lives so we can take the necessary steps from *within* to remove them permanently.

PEARL #34

Conflicts Reside Where There Is Incorrect Understanding

Who or what is the culprit of conflicts? Ignorance!

In actuality, where is there any such thing as conflicts in this world? Conflicts means simply erred understanding. Wherever there is a lack of correct understanding, there are conflicts; in every place there is a lack of correct understanding, there is pain and suffering. There is actually no such thing as pain and suffering whatsoever either. The pain, it is pain due to the dogmatic lack of intention to understanding correctly.

To sit in the house with a sulky face, that is called *turmoil*. It is an insignificant type of conflict that then becomes a huge fiasco. With these ridiculous dividing differences and conflicts the human life acquired at such a huge price gets wasted. Whatever "time" is spent engaging in conflicts that much "time" is bound in animal life form! Time spent in *healing* does not bind animal life form.

Insights From Pearl #34

When we realize and accept our greatest enemies are *within* in the form of anger, pride, illusion, greed driven by misguided ego; that is when our understanding will find truth. Then we will begin to cultivate virtues such as humility, honesty, courage, inner strength, kindness, forgiveness, patience and the list goes on as we discover the treasures that reside in the heart center. Power of intention is what makes us human beings and differentiates us from other life forms. Ignorance is not bliss! We must not waste away this precious, fleeting human life without getting the correct understanding as to the art of living a meaningful, harmonious life with joy and peace as driving forces.

PEARL #35

With Correct Understanding Conflicts Are Disposed

Humans are miserable because of wrongful understanding, due to seeking-out understanding from others there is misery. If the quest to seek understanding were not taken, this wrongful understanding would never have arisen. Suffering, it is all the resulting manifestation of erred understanding. Within oneself in one's own mind one believes, *'I know this, and I know that.'* Fool, what is it that you have known? Despite knowing so much your disputes with the wife have not subsided. If on someday there is a disagreement with the wife, you have no knowledge of how to bring a resolution to it; your faces remain sulky for fifteen days at a time. He will ask, 'How can I resolve it?' The one who does not even know how to resolve a disagreement with his wife, what can he be capable of understanding about heart-centered humane inner living (*dharma*)? If there is a disagreement with the neighbor, he is incapable of resolving it, what good is that? The art of conflict resolution should be known, right?

Like these big shot judges that sentence people to seven years jail time at–a–time on a regular day had come in contact with me and the disagreements with their wives their "cases" at home are still left unresolved "pending" to this day! I told them, 'Why do you not bring resolution to those "cases" at home first! The police "cases" are not a big deal.' But, how can they clear the mess up at home? They do not have an understanding or know–how of this, right! They do not have an understanding of how to resolve differences that arise with the wife, right! Human beings do not have an understanding of how to resolve these disputes, so time does the job for them. Otherwise, by themselves, at the present moment, right away one should "adjust", these people unfortunately do not have that understanding.

Questioner – They do not even know how to take a U–turn and make amends.

Dadashri – No, but they simply just do not understand, then how can they back peddle and turn things around? Then, "time" does the job of bringing a resolution. At long last, "time" brings an end to each and every thing at some point.

Insights From Pearl #35

Winning the home is winning the world! If there is no peace, harmony and true affection at home, it does not matter if there are millions in the world who sing one's praises. The true worth of a human being is whether those in the home will give a no objection certificate. When we cannot find resolution within ourselves, how can we find it with anyone else?! It all starts with number one. No matter how big a hat we may wear in the world professionally or as a business person, the real gage for the art of living is with those closest to us in the home. If we cannot satisfy the hearts and minds of those in the home, what good is our life as a human being? Home is truly where the heart is.

Even a foster child raised without parents will never forget that someone abandoned them for whatever reason. Those scars in the heart will remain unresolved and pending until they find true healing from correct understanding. They will always harbor a desire to know who their parents were and why they left them. The heart does not forget matters pertaining to the heart and until healing takes place; there is no peace or resolution of conflict within.

It behooves us to carefully examine all of our close relations and concentrate on healthy dialogue, forgiveness, and making amends to remove animosity of any sort. It is truly in our best interest as it ensures living our life with little or no regrets at the end of the day. Human life is a fleeting gift in the vast expanse of time as it is! Why let a moment be wasted?!?

PEARL #36

Living Together In The Home And So Why Conflicts?

Questioner – My wife and I do not get along at all! No matter how innocent my talk is, even if what I am is saying is true; she will still take it the wrong way. Living with friction with forces outside the home goes on; but what is this friction with this lady about?

Dadashri – It is like this, a person mentally and emotionally abuses someone under their care and protection. This someone who is dependent on them, to such an extent that they leave no stone unturned in this abuse. If a person comes under their hand, is dependent on them, whether a man or a woman; under their authority they are merciless in harassing that person leaving nothing to the imagination.

There should never without exception be any disturbing noisy conflict with the people in the home. What use is disturbing noisy conflict with those that share the same roof? By harassing another it will never happen that oneself one will realize peace and happiness. And we must give kindness, affection, love, caring to others to receive it back ourselves. Only if we give what brings others joy, peace and bliss in the home then we get it back; and the tea, refreshments and snacks will be made well and served, if not even they will be made badly and served badly.

The weak, pathetic husband holds a butchers knife over the wife! How can we destroy those under our own shelter?! Those who have come under the shelter of our hands should be protected that should be our greatest of all goals, even if they have made gross mistakes they should still be protected. Those soldiers that are prisoners of, even they are kept under such careful protection, right?! Well, these are those in our very own home, are they not!? In this, outside with others they will be like purring kittens, there they will not create quarrels with anyone and all this ridiculous lunacy at home only. Those under one's own authority are harassed, abused and broken–down to pieces and the bosses are applauded with respect.

Right now, if the police come and interrogate him with questions, he will behave with humility and respect and at home if the "wife" is telling truly beneficial and wise things, he cannot bear it and instead humiliates her. He shakes–up everyone in the home by yelling things like, 'How did this ant get in my tea cup?' Instead why do you not just peacefully remove it, huh! Terrorizing those at home and pathetically petrified in front of the police!!

Now, this is called a gross injustice. This does not become us. The lady is our partner in and for our life. Are there conflicts with the life partner? In this where there are conflicts arising some pathways to resolution must be found, understanding must be adopted. If you want to stay in the home; then why do so with conflicts?

Insights From Pearl #36

None of us are perfect. If we were, we would not be here. We are here on this earth to become better *human* beings. We are here to cultivate and grow in our humanity. What better purpose is there than to become better? There is no one on this earth who has not made mistakes and does not have weaknesses. So, those in our homes, they are part of our life team. We cannot ever treat any member of our team badly! Rather, if we empower them, we ourselves become empowered to be better. The home should be a place where we find comfort, solace, unconditional acceptance and true affection. How else can it be called "home"? Encouraging and kind words hold power to empower others. It all begins with us. Our presence can project it if we have it *within* us. So, it behooves us to cultivate virtues *within* us that can empower ourselves and others with a life that is beautiful and meaningful. Challenges then become opportunities to rise to the occasion rather than destroying what means the most to us. If we do not value ourselves enough to cultivate virtues then how can we value anyone else?

PEARL #37

Salute To The Home Where There Are No Conflicts

Dadashri – Those that spend their whole lives in noisy disturbing conflicts, both go to hell.

Questioner – If one of the two has been blessed with '*gyan*' (initiated with divine knowledge of self) then what?

Dadashri – They get a clue. Then the other spinning top (spouse) slows down and softens too. Since, there is no "reaction" from the other side, *softening* happens. Then, that one *too* gets liberated. But, where both are engaged actively in noisy disturbing conflicts *neither* will ever be liberated from the cycle of birth–n–death.

Questioner – That is why *Krupalu Dev* (Shrimad Rajchandra) has written that He offered His *namaskar* to any home that is without conflicts for even a single day.

Dadashri – Yes, *namaskar.*

Questioner – For those who have not taken '*gyan*' (been initiated with divine knowledge), at those homes where conflicts do not arise, what is that called?

Dadashri – That is called like demi–gods, but that is just not possible in this day–n–age of age of clash and conflict! Because those conflicts that are present, they spread like a contagious viral disease. Like a plague spreads, it has the same impact. Each and every home has been plagued by conflicts!

Questioner – What is the difference between the indifference to conflicts that someone who does not have '*gyan*' versus someone who does?

Dadashri – The one without '*gyan*' has an intellectually–driven indifference to conflicts and after '*gyan*' (knowledge of self) that indifference to conflicts arises *spontaneously,* the sense of *doer–ship* falls off.

Questioner – Can it be that there is not a single instance of a conflict–free home on any given day?

Dadashri – Now imagine that there may be one, however, he is a doer himself. He is continually actively planning and strategizing; suppose there are four people in the home and if one *trouble–maker* slips into the home, then eventually the *trouble* will spread to conflicts amongst everyone in the home.

Insights From Pearl #37

The one who understands the damage that conflicts cause in the home, driven by that ego, intellectually strives to keep conflicts out of the home. This involves doer-ship because it is ego-driven. In today's day-and-age of clash and conflict, it is almost impossible to find a home truly without conflicts. We are entwined into the web of a conflict-driven world and it can permeate from so many avenues. It takes tremendous awareness and vigilance to remain free from conflict with or without self-realization in today's world. However, this cannot be used as an excuse. If we believe in re-incarnation, who wants to go to hell? We would aspire to come back as human beings so we can further develop ourselves to the ultimate goal of eternal bliss and freedom at the very least! We cannot give up in our quest for attaining the correct understanding of the art of living human life. Even if we do not believe in re-incarnation, who wants to live a miserable conflict-ridden life? The art of living applies to everyone regardless of beliefs about re-incarnation (liberation from the cycle of birth-n-death).

PEARL #38

Authentic Heart-Centered Inner Living Is Conflict–Free

The places where there are no conflicts, there it is true religion and truly humane society. Where there is authenticity in religion, there cannot be conflicts. At each and every home there are conflicts happening. So, where did the religions go? For the sheer purpose of getting through worldly living, religion is required to learn what to do in order to steer clear of conflicts; if only that is learned it is considered as having *mastered* religion. To live a life without any conflicts that itself *is* religion.

In *Hindustan*, in this worldly life one's own home should be like a blissful heavenly abode, if not, should it not at least come close to that? It should be *free* from conflicts. That is why the Scriptures (*Shashtras*) have said that where there is even the slightest inkling of conflict, there is not any heart-centered inner living. It should be such if the environment is like a "jail" there is no "depression" or if the environment is like a palace there is no "elevation". When life becomes such that it is without any conflicts means one is close at–hand to liberation and that one surely gets *blissful* from within in the same lifetime. Each and every one wants liberation (*moksha*) as no one likes bondage, but if you become *totally* conflict–free then know that the station for liberation (*moksha*) is mighty close.

We became self–realized with 'Gyan' in 1958, and have been absolutely conflict–free for the last twenty years, but even the twenty years prior to 'Gyan' (eternal knowledge) we did not ever have even the slightest bit of conflict. From childhood, we had literally thrown out conflict. For any reason or cause, we realized it was not worth it to create conflicts in this world.

The *Lord* has said when focused heart-centered inner living is present; it is conflict free at that place there are no conflicts. There may be more or less money, but life should be conflict–free. To find a conflict–free home like this is a terribly difficult task. Differences of opinion are called conflicts and where there are conflicts worldly life continues to stand. Whoever has broken free from conflicts can be counted as having attained status of the *Lord*.

Insights From Pearl #38

The *Lord* has said that, "100% human means the *Lord* Himself." So, it is a worthy *goal* to have even if it cannot be accomplished in this lifetime, we can keep it in our mind's eye as our goal so nature can help us move in that direction by bringing the appropriate spiritual guides and teachers in our path. The true definition of wealth is something that is definitely worth investigating and defining for ourselves from *within*. A big, pure and open heart makes someone far richer than someone who has money but is unable to share it. A loving, kind and compassionate heart is far more valuable than excessive monetary riches and luxuries that bring one nothing but mental strain, physical ailments and a hectic lifestyle. In this day-n-age of excess, *less is more*, which means more affection, kindness, compassion, open communication, productive dialogue and ultimately meaningful, purposeful living!

Conflicts Are Unbecoming To Those Who Are Civilized

Questioner – Here in America women work as well right, so women come into increased "power", so "husband–wife" end up in amplified bickering.

Dadashri – It's actually better if there is "power", we should comprehend that wow she who was "power"–less before, that she has come into "power" is really nice for us! The cart runs well, does it not? The oxen that pull the carts, is it better if they are weak or powerful?

Questioner – But, if they display false "power" then does it not run poorly? If "power" is utilized constructively then it is good.

Dadashri – It is like this, if there is no receiver for the show of "power", then it just hits the walls. She could be showing off this way or that way, but if the water in our belly stays calm and cool, then her "power" hits the walls and bounces back again to hit her only.

Questioner – So, are you really trying to tell us that we should not listen to what the spouses say?

Dadashri – Listen, listen to all of it *mindfully*, all that is said that is advantageous and beneficial listen diligently; and if the "power" starts blowing hot air, at those times remain totally silent. So, we just observe how much she has drunk (intoxication from egotistical doer-ship)! Her display of "power" will be according to the amount of her consumption, right?

Questioner 2 – That is correct. Then in the same way when men use false "power" what then?

Dadashri – Then we need to stay focused. Realizing that today he is *really* losing it, then tell yourself from within, 'Do not say anything out loud'. Stay silent.

Questioner 2 – Oh I see, if not he will lose control all the more.

Dadashri – You understand that today, he has lost control over his mind. Really speaking, it should not happen this way. It is so beautiful; would two friends ever behave in such a way? Will that beautiful friendship survive, if such things are done? Hence, these two are called friends in actuality; woman–man means the home is to be run based on the workings and foundation of true friendship.

And it has been degraded to this level; do you think people get their daughters married for *this* to green card holders? So they can do all this *nonsense*? Then, what does this make us look great? What do you think? This is not flattering at all to us! What can be called civilized? If there are conflicts in the home is that called civilized or if there are no conflicts?

Questioner – After all, how can this be? We are civilized, educated people.

Insights From Pearl #39

Active listening involves utilizing the mind and the heart. When we listen from the heart center, we can decipher exactly what the other person is trying to tell us. Perhaps, they are just tired, or need some tender loving care or simply want to be validated. If we listen from a place of humanity, the messages that the apparently caustic words are conveying can be easily comprehended. So, in the name of peace, harmony and equanimity, we can administer the appropriate medication. Silence speaks much louder than words when we cannot find our center from within. The other person will appreciate our silence when they come down from their rants.

Civilized does not mean eating with forks and knives and sitting on fancy leather sofas in style. Truly to be civilized and educated means knowing the art of true affection, caring, and conflict resolution amicably by active heart-centered listening with others. When someone close to us is having a difficult, uncontrolled moment, why would we want to add fuel to the fire? That is namely uncivilized. Rather shower them with the pure waters of compassion that can only flow from the heart center through empathy with the other person.

True friendship means forgiving and forgetting on a daily basis. There is no need to carry-forward anything when we have whole-heartedly accepted that person as a friend for life and living. The bond that is shared with a true friend has no bearing on circumstances; it is a matter of the heart and oneness of hearts.

When we decide to share our lives with another person, it does not mean we are out to change that person. Sharing is caring and caring is sharing. Our only purpose is to share our lives and ourselves with that person. There must be appropriate boundaries of respect and honor in any relationship.

PEARL #40

Blow Away Conflicts Altogether

So, please do ask all the "common" questions. Do ask, without any reservation, all the pertinent questions pertaining to your worldly life. Please do ask about the "common" things. In the "common" there is not too much trouble. Even if there are conflicts arising in the home, despite this how to blow them away forever, *ask that*!

Question – So conflicts do not arise, what to do for that?

What is the appropriate pathway for that?

Dadashri – Tell me what are the things that cause conflicts, and then I can immediately show you the prescription for those things causing conflicts to arise.

Questioner – They happen for matters relating to money, matters relating to the children, conflicts arise for everything, even for the most ridiculous irrelevant little things cause conflicts to happen.

Dadashri – What happens in money matters?

Questioner – Money is not being saved and it all gets spent.

Dadashri – So how is it the husband's fault in this?

Questioner – There is no fault on his part. Sometimes, quarrels happen because of this.

Dadashri – So, do not engage in conflicts. If two hundred dollars get spent even then do not start conflicts, because the value of conflicts is worth four hundred dollars. If two hundred dollars get spent the conflicts result in spending double that amount; and to create four hundred dollars worth of conflicts it is smarter to let the two hundred dollars go bye–bye, then do not engage in conflicts to top it off. After all, the rise–n–fall of dollars is in the hands of settlement of karmic accounts according to nature's forces in the cosmic universe.

By engaging in noisy disturbing conflicts money does not grow. In this, if merit karmas ripen, it just does not take long at all for money to multiply. So, if money is being used in excess (*in your opinion*) then do not bicker about it, because that which is gone is gone; rather by the conflicts that are created, forget the excess fifty that got spent, conflicts worth a hundred get *spent*. So, conflicts should never be created ever *as a rule*.

First of all conflicts should not happen at all in the home, and if they do arise *by chance* they should be immediately resolved. If slight signs of impending conflicts arising that an inferno could ensue, instantly water should be poured to cool things down metaphorically speaking. To live a life filled with conflicts like the old days, what benefit is there in that? What is the point of it? There certainly should not be a life full of conflicts right? What is going to be rationed–out and taken with us? In the home, you all eat and drink beverages together so of what use is disturbing noisy conflict? And if someone says something bad about the husband then she gets pissed–off that how could they say such a thing? And she will insult him herself, 'You are like this. You are like that.' All this should not be. Even the husband should not do this. If you have conflicts between you, all this it affects the children badly. So, conflicts *must* go. When the conflicts go from the home, the children, too, become their best. In this nonsense all the children have become their worst!

Insights From Pearl #40

Our children learn what they live and breathe every day in the home. They also learn from the outside world, but it is up to us to give them the foundation in the *home* to be able to deal with the myriad challenges that life with undoubtedly show them along the raging river of life. If we are not setting an example through our behavior with each other, where will they learn effective conflict resolution and how to live in harmony with other human beings? If we argue and bicker over small things, they will lose total respect for us. They will assume we do not know anything about life and tune us out altogether. When we validate and encourage each other; forgive and give each other solace; value the feelings and thoughts of each other; show each other true affection; then the children learn what they see and feel in their hearts. Human beings learn as they see and feel in the heart center.

PEARL #41

Conflicts Happening; Is It A Result Of The Outcome Of Past Karmas Or Ignorance?

Questioner – Is it due to the outcome of past karmas manifesting that noisy disturbing conflicts happen?

Dadashri – No, it arises due to ignorance, conflict! When conflicts arise, in that, all new seeds of karmas are being planted. Manifestation of past karmas as *happenings* is not inclusive of conflicts arising.

Questioner – You mean past karmas manifesting does not include conflicts?

Dadashri – That is impossible, it can *never* be! Due to ignorance, oneself how one should conduct oneself *here–n–now* is not known that is why conflicts happen. So then there is no reason whatsoever for any turmoil right!

In this, due to the darkness of ignorance there is inner turmoil. Conflicts mean ignorance. Due to ignorance, all the conflicts stand. As ignorance goes, conflicts get pushed far away.

Questioner – So, before conflicts have a chance to arise we should quickly see the happenings of karmic results manifesting.

Dadashri – It is not a question of seeing. If we are a part of it, then we should know it for what it is as it is. What is that, who am I, what is all this, all should be known, in a brief *instantaneous* way. If there is a clay pot, and that clay pot if the little boy breaks it, even then the husband does not get mad at anyone in the home; and if the little boy breaks a big expensive *Mikasa* vase then? What does the husband say to the wife? He will say, 'You are not watching him properly.' That poor zombie, why did he not say anything about the clay pot? Because it is worthless to him, it has no value. If there is no value we do not create conflicts and only in matters of value to us we create conflicts right! Both things are due to the manifestation of karmic results, that they break, but what is the reason we do not create conflicts about the clay pot? Hence, conflicts are not due to the manifestation of karmic results, they are due to the darkness of ignorance.

Questioner – Yes, it is due to ignorance! But for conflicts to arise is there some initiating activity, is it not some mentally–driven process?

Dadashri – Conflicts are a result of psychological mental issues, but what does it mean that they are due to ignorance? In this if one person loses two–thousand rupees, and then he gets plagued by mental worry and anxiety. Then if that same thing happens to someone else, they lose two thousand rupees. Then, that person may react differently saying that it must have been due to his past karmas. See, if there is that knowledge, if that understanding is present then it gets resolved! Otherwise, conflicts are not from past lives, are not due to karmas resulting of the past. Conflicts are the bitter fruits of seeds of ignorance.

Questioner – "Exactly", both of them lose two thousand despite this one of them has no inner turmoil over it.

Dadashri – So many people lose two thousand rupees and remain unaffected, does that happen or not? Then, on the other hand, there are so many that get terribly affected at losing two thousand rupees do you know this? So, suffering is not due to the fruits of past karmas manifesting now. Pain, suffering and turmoil, are nothing but the bitter fruit of our seeds of ignorance planted in the past.

Insights From Pearl #41

The core culprit for any conflicts in life is ignorance. We cannot ever assume that conflict is meant to be. Conflict is something that will cause new karmic seeds to be planted. When the understanding from *within* is not positively illuminated, it results in conflict. First-and-foremost we must understand ourselves! 'Know Thyself,' as present-day Holistic Guide Kanudadaji tells us with such pure affection. We must know our own mind and inner dialogue to understand our own nature. We must have a solid self-esteem for who we are first. Then only, we can really understand another person. People are far more valuable than things, then why does our behavior not demonstrate that? It is because we have not truly understood this as a fact of *experience*. It cannot hurt us to just try putting people before things and begin to gain the wisdom of experience that this practice provides to us.

PEARL #42

By Resonating Positively, Noisy Drama Subsides

Questioner – Suppose someone purposely threw this thing away, then what "adjustment" should be taken on our part in such a case?

Dadashri – So the thing gets thrown–out by someone, but even if someone's son is purposely thrown out we should just watch. If the father throws out the son we should just watch! Well, what are we supposed to throw out the husband? One has already ended–up in the hospital, now should we get two in the hospital? And when he gets in the mood, he throws around the wife, and then three have been hospitalized at that point.

Questioner – Then, what do not say anything at all?

Dadashri – Say something, but highlight the positive if you know how to say it, if not what is the point in barking like dogs? Thus, say something that resonates positively with the other person.

Questioner – Resonates positively meaning in what way?

Dadashri – 'Oh my goodness! Why did you throw the boy? For what reason?' Then he will say, 'Would I do this on purpose? He just got jerked out of my hands and got thrown out!'

Questioner – But this is a lie he is telling right?

Dadashri – We do not need to see that he is lying. Whether he lies or tells the truth it is up to him that is not in our power. He will do whatever he feels like doing! If he wants to lie or if he even wants to kill us that is his problem. In the middle of the night at 2 am if he puts poison in our water then we would certainly die right! Hence, what is not within our power we do need to worry about or be paranoid. It is useful if empathetic speech is learned, 'Dear, what benefit was doing this for you?' Then, he will confess on his own. You are not speaking empathetically and if you give him five mouthfuls of spiteful speech, he will give you back ten.

Questioner – If we do not know *how* to tell him anything, then what should we do? Sit quietly with mouths shut?

Dadashri – Stay silent and keep watching 'What is happening?' When the kids in the movie theater make noise, what do we do? We have the right to tell everyone, but in a manner that does not escalate the noisy drama. Otherwise, if telling increases the disturbing noisy conflicts, it is the work of idiots.

Insights From Pearl #42

If we cannot bring peace with our words that must come from the heart, then it is best to remain silent and simply observe the happenings. This is not to be misused. If we see injustice occurring, it is certainly up to us to speak up in an appropriate manner. But, it must be without any insistence because we cannot control others behavior. We can make our position known in a very quiet and gentle manner. However, of utmost importance is to keep the conflict from escalating. And if that means being silent and quietly watching the happenings, then that is in our best interest and those around us. Barking at each other like dogs is not the way to effective conflict resolution by any means! It is not up to us to be the judge, jury and lawyer all together in the case. We simply must have the goal to bring peaceful resolution for all those involved without hurting anyone in the process.

PEARL #43

The Root Of Pain & Suffering Is Self Ignorance

There are so many people who do not have life insurance, despite this their faces light up and they are able to stay quiet on the outside and stay peaceful on the inside as well; on the other hand there are so many who show–out turmoil, anguish and pain from inside-and-out. The root cause being ignorance and mistaken understanding! It was going to ignite; there is no surprise about it at all. Even if the head is blown to bits to death, even so it is not going to change anything.

Questioner – To maintain a positive attitude about resulting happenings is that not considered in the jurisdiction of the mind?

Dadashri – To take things "positively" is the realm of the mind, but even so only if there is 'gyan' (eternal knowledge) then only it is taken with a "positive" attitude, otherwise it will be viewed as "negative" only, right! This whole world is miserable. Like fish flipping about out–of–water gasping for air, despite owning mills! Thus, there is a serious urgent need to understand this correctly.

The art of living human life needs to be known. There is, of course, an art to living human life right! Not everyone is ready for liberation (*moksha*), but there should at least be the art of living human life right! It is okay to have illusory infatuation (*moha*), but with that illusory infatuation at least know the art of living life; that how to go about living life. There is all this frenzy for seeking pleasure, so is there pleasure in conflicts? Conflicts, in fact, bring pain even in delightful fun. All this roaming is in search of fun and it only brings pain. If the art of living human life is known, then pain does not follow. If there is suffering and pain, then the art of living human life throws it out.

Times of conflicts are passed through one way or another, but during that time infinite lives are bound for oneself. From infinite lives the seeds of conflict have been hoarded and sowed, when that tide comes in conflicts swell like a tsunami. The *'Gyani Purush'* takes those bags full of seeds of conflict and burns them to ashes, and then conflicts cease to arise. *Shrimad Rajchandra* had said that, 'I offer *namaskar* to whomever's home a single day passes without conflicts!'

Insights From Pearl #43

A positive inner attitude with gratitude is the greatest gift anyone can give themselves! It has to be cultivated within in order to become a habit, a good habit that allows common sense to blossom. There are the few if any on this earth who have the personal inner strength and will power to accomplish this on their own! The enlightened spiritual guide must be sought-out who can show the way. Then, with your own conviction and His grace it happens *spontaneously*. No matter what one's needs and wants are in life, the way to accomplish them should not lead to suffering and misery. Then, what is the point of living this precious gift of human life? The Holistic Master Guide is tried and tested in the art of humane inner living and can show the way no matter what level the personal goal. Human life is but a fleeting moment in the vast expanse of time. Why allow it to be wasted away in suffering and misery? Invest in yourself!

PEARL #44

A True Guru Is One Who Removes Conflicts

A guru is the one that makes us understand what will stop us from having conflicts. A whole month of conflict free living is a great indicator of our caliber of understanding, and one who gives us this knowledge is can be called a guru. If we still have conflicts then we should understand we have not met a true guru. What is the use of having a guru if inner turmoil, agitation and confusion persist within and with others?

A guru can be called the one of whom we have devotion with correct understanding, and we have surrendered all of our sense of doer–ship to him, otherwise how can he be a guru? If our darkness is pushed far away by walking down the road he has shown us; and anger–pride–illusion–greed gradually decrease, differences of opinion gradually subside, and worries and conflicts do not happen whatsoever; then we have achieved our goal---no conflicts. If conflicts happen, ignorance still prevails!

Insights From Pearl #44

Our hearts will tell us and the results within our own being will tell us if a guru is right for us. We must learn to listen to our heart center. If our inner life is not becoming more peaceful, blissful and serene, then that guru may not be the right one for us. If we experience an increase in anger, pride, deceit and greed despite having surrendered to a guru then that guru may not be the one who can liberate us. We must use this as a thermometer. The quality of our life *within* us should gradually become better, more blissful, more peaceful, more balanced; then we can gage that this guru is the right one for us.

PEARL #45

Upon Meeting The True Guru Conflicts Go

In this, conflicts are not going, weaknesses are not going and he will say 'I have found a guru.' If conflicts stop in our home, loud noisy drama stops, that can be called having found a guru, if not, how can it be called having found a guru!? Or else all those so–called gurus are doing is putting up another membership card in your name as another follower. So, they use this card and drive you with it. The ego that you give to identify with some other belief system, they turn it to their tune. If we met a true guru for even six months, then he would at least teach something that would make conflicts go away in the home. Not just in the home, but even the inner conflicts of the mind would go. If the mind does not become turmoil–free and if conflicts continue to happen then that guru should be abandoned. Then, find another guru.

Insights From Pearl #45

Conflict resolution is really the reason most people seek-out a guru. They are seeking peace within themselves and want to put an end to the inner turmoil. If the inner turmoil persists, there is definitely a problem with the choice. We must know our boundaries as to what is best for us. If that surrender leads to more distress and turmoil, there is a problem somewhere. We have not obtained the correct understanding from the guru or the guru is not what he is claiming to be. The guru is responsible for the one who has surrendered regardless in the grand scheme of Mother Nature and will have to answer to nature's laws for any shortcomings and misdeeds. If we are not getting resolution within and finding answers to our questions to our satisfaction, there is valid reason to abandon.

PEARL #46

The Enlightened Spiritual Guide (Gyani) Makes One Free From Conflicts

No one in the world can free one from conflicts. Only the *"Gyani Purush"* alone can free people from conflicts.

You are of such a mature age, so you have found a solution right?

Questioner – No, Dada, I am telling as a matter of truth.

Dadashri – With me everyone tells the truth, but conflicts must be removed right, a resolution must be accomplished right!

Question – Yes, they do have to be removed.

Dadashri – Now, whatever you do, do it mindfully! Put *Dada* the *Lord's* name into it. That I am doing everything in the name of *Dada* the *Lord*. If you take the name of *Dada the Lord* then instantly your wish will be granted, conflicts will die.

If she (wife) does not create conflicts, then you do not either right!

Questioner – Then, I do not initiate them.

Dadashri – Yes, then that is enough. Fine, both have found resolution.

"Educated" people these days fight more at home!

What can be called "educated"? That from morning until night time, there is not even by chance the slightest tad of conflict in the home.

Questioner – Then does it not happen that only one "party" continually has to do the understanding and the other one continually "dominates", then is that not like a "one way" thing?

Dadashri – No, that does not happen. Both eventually get it and you should gently converse about it. Say that it seems I have fully understood this and you still seem to be struggling to understand so let us fully understand what *Dadaji* says together. So, we never get into arguments ever again, and live conflict–free like *Dada* had said.

The home where there are no conflicts, The *Lord* resides without fail, The *Lord* does not move from there. If on some blue moon, a slip happens and a conflict arises, then both should sit together and repent in the name of the *Lord*, resolving not to let it happen again. We made a mistake, so please do not get up from here. We tell the *Lord* never to leave from now on.

Insights From Pearl #46

As present Holistic Guide Kanudadashri says, "Educate the educator." We must educate the educator *within* who has erroneous understanding. The understanding must be turned to a correct upright position. The negative inner dialogue must be countered with the correct positive inner dialogue through inner awareness and alertness.

We do not gain education in the relative world to make our lives more difficult! That is not the purpose of education. Education is so we can learn to live better, more peacefully, more harmoniously and with more joy and affection for others; ultimately a more satisfying life in general.

What is the purpose of an education that causes a family to break? What kind of education is *that*? That cannot be called education. Dadaji's Mahatmas have had their problems solved by His grace. Their lives are not *perfect*, but they are not conflict-ridden either! Mahatmas have been given the in simple English words of timeless wisdom such as "Adjust Everywhere" and "Avoid Clashes" to bring balance back when a Mahatma gets knocked off their center.

Furthermore, the Nine Priceless Diamonds are priceless to those who truly want to live a meaningful, purpose-driven human life while on this earth. The Nine Priceless Diamonds when sincerely integrated into one's inner intentions from the heart center hold the power to lighten the load of even the heaviest of karmic loads. The Nine Priceless Diamonds are designed to integrate a peaceful and harmonious mode of living to be and continually grow in one's humanity.

PEARL #47

If Conflicts Stop Then A Complete Solution

It is like this, in this world conflicts and noisy drama, on the basis of these two this world stands. If this conflict and noisy drama stop in our home then perhaps some solutions to the world problems can be found. We surveyed many of our *Mahatmas* with regards to conflicts–noisy drama in their homes, when we ask them they say, 'There are no conflicts left now. If it seems they may arise, we put them out before they have a chance to ignite, so it is barely even noticeable that they happen to others.'

In one month if only two days a conflict arises that is plenty. Conflicts–noisy drama should not be present in the world. If we ask our *Mahatmas* in Ahmedabad, so many homes that are conflict–free, noisy drama–free will be found there!

Insights From Pearl #47

All human beings on earth ultimately seek bliss. No one enjoys the anguish and misery that darkness of ignorance brings with it. Mahatmas that have met, understood and surrendered to the *Gyani Purush* (Enlightened Spiritual Guide) are extremely fortunate and hold very high merit karmic deeds to have done so. It is their priceless fortune of earnings of many lives in the form of a horn of plenty! To find a "complete solution" is no small feat in this misery-filled human existence on this earth at this particular point in time. It is a miracle!

PEARL #48

When Conflicts Are Broken, That Itself Is Liberation

In a conflict–filled environment, the one who does not have even the slightest conflict within or with anyone else, that namely is *moksha*. Conflict–filled environments will continue to come. Does the sun not shine? If the doors are held will they stop banging anyways? That just goes on. If doors are swinging then just stand a little farther away. If there were not conflict–filled environments, how would bliss (*mukti*) be tasted? *Dada's* liberation (*moksha*) is such that conflict–filled scenes invade from every direction, despite this, bliss (*mukti*) persists.

The *Lord* has not said anything is 'bondage', eating–drinking beverages, that is all natural behavior of the relative personality, but when the conflict of the soul breaks that only in itself is bliss (*mukti*), the breaking of conflicts in itself only is..... liberation (*moksha*).

At any given time no matter what type of happenings come around, despite this conflicts do not arise then you have mastered all the *Shashtras* (scriptures) in their entirety. Outside any kinds of happenings can come and they may even make you feel like vomiting, and the closer it comes in your face and appears repeatedly and can be seen clearly conflict arises *within*, despite this if an inferno does not erupt you have mastered the all the holy scriptures (*Shashtras*). Even between guru and student conflicts arise!

After meeting the *Gyani Purush* in the midst of myriad conflict–filled environments, conflicts still will not arise right! What kind of a '*gyan*' has this '*Dada*' given these *Mahatmas*?! Under no conditions will conflicts arise and that attachment–free bliss persists! The breaking of conflicts is namely bliss (*mukti*), here–and–now bliss (*mukti*) has manifested itself.

Insights From Pearl #48

It does not happen overnight in all cases. Where the karmic loads are heavy, it can take more time. It is a process of inner cleansing as old karmas from the past get emptied-out. The transformation takes place from *inside-outward*. The most beautiful and amazing thing about this holistic inner science is that it does not require anything from the aspiring seeker except correct understanding and awareness. There is no "doing" or "renouncing" here.

Even without being initiated with self-realization, one can introspectively make the firm decision and conviction to break conflict once and for all from within. This will allow the universe to bring the scientific circumstantial evidences together to bring that to a manifestation. The inner intent and firm conviction for wanting to become conflict-free is the platinum key.

Apology For Hurtful Speech

Questioner – Against our will despite this if conflicts happen, spiteful, caustic words escape our mouths then what should be done?

Dadashri – The habits or actions that are close to stopping keep happening despite our not wanting them to, so when they do happen anyways *at that time* engage in serious heartfelt repentance–apology for it from within.

Questioner – We may resolve within our mind that we do not want to talk to that person, we do not want to make any trouble, do not want to fight; and despite it all, some weird little thing happens that a fight ensues again with them, cannot help saying something again, conflicts happen. Everything awful itself happens. What should I do at that time to prevent this vicious cycle?

Dadashri – It is on its last *"steps"*, when the end of a road has come close, then even though we have no intent whatsoever *wrong* happens, then what should we do there? That through *sincere* repentance it gets *erased*, that is all. If wrong happens this is the only solution, there is no other solution. That too when that bad habit is close to coming to an end the intent to do it is *void* and it still happens, if not then that bad habit is still half–way, we would still have the inner intent to do it and the bad habit happens as well, *both* happen. The inner intent to not do all these wrongs yet the wrongs still happen, then you can know their days are numbered, they are nearing their end. From this, the end can be discerned, so "*coming events cast their shadows before.*"

Whatever gets spoken gets repented for so you get absolved from responsibility! Speak austerely, but speak words without attachment–detachment from within. If severely harsh words get spoken then *immediately* engage in sincere apology and repentance from *within*.

Insights From Pearl #49

Anxiety, turmoil and stress invade our psyche from every direction in today's hustling and bustling world. To keep our attention *inward* and focused in the center requires tremendous vigilance, focus and conviction. When the inner balance is lost, then vomiting can occur. Vomiting in the form of spiteful, caustic and hurtful words that one could not find resolution for within oneself. At this time, the *Gyani Purush* has given us the priceless tool of confession, apology, repentance and resolve not to commit again from within. Of course, the more sincere and heartfelt it is, the more absolved we are from our transgression from normality. Through His grace, if the conviction is strong enough, we will be free from these bad habits as they are no longer endorsed by us or given support by us. Eventually, they will have to exhaust themselves out!

When we move the sofa, everything under it gets cleaned up. We must move ourselves away from the bad habit and internally continually stand-up to what we know is destructive to our lives. The final steps in climbing a mountain can be the most rigorous and sacrificial. But, when we reach the apex, it all becomes worth our time and effort. The beauty of this science is that 'we' do not have to 'do' any climbing or take any of these efforts, we simply must keep the firm conviction and unwavering focus on the goal to become conflict-free from within for the sake of our own inner bliss!

PEARL #50

Conflicts, Even After Acquiring Wisdom?!

Whoever does not have any conflict arising within the mind; their worldly life has arrived at its sunset!

The mind free from conflicts is '*moksha*' (liberated). The mind with conflicts is '*sansar*' (worldly relative life).

Questioner – Sometimes, the mind becomes conflict–filled, what is the reason for this?

Dadashri – What is happening to the mind, we just need to *observe* it. You yourself do not go into the mind, do not get immersed in it, the mind is a thing to be seen and known, all of the thoughts the mind generates are to be seen and known, they are all subtle circumstances of which you are the *knower–perceiver*. Now, what at all is left to be touched on in this? In this, if the right button is not known and a small mistake is made the fan starts up on a cold winter day, but once it is known for what it is, then it is fine again.

That is not called conflict at all; it is just a little shakiness of the mind. The mind naturally has hiccups, which is not called conflict, so just keep watching it.

Questioner – So, if we just keep observing the mind, then does that mean thoughts have stopped?

Dadashri – We are just to observe whether they have stopped or not stopped. What is observed does not touch us. Like this torch, if this torch is burning, if we observe it does it burn our eyes? Well, does it not burn if we look at it? By observing nothing happens to us, if you stick your finger in the flame then it will burn. This is a bad thought; if it gets acknowledged and endorsed as such then it does leave its mark.

So, observe the thoughts that come in the mind *too*, even the good thoughts that come just *observe*. Bad thoughts and good thoughts are based on social expectations, not on the basis of the *Lord's* expectations. According to the *Lord*, the mind is functioning according to its own innate nature. When the mind thinks, *bad* or *good*, or *indifferently*, then the fact that it is the mind has been *verified* from within without a doubt.

Insights From Pearl #50

The mind is a physical thing. It is made-up of grey matter and has the subtle aspects as a part-n-parcel of the whole intricate nervous system within the body. The synapses of the nerves and dendrites are all a naturally occurring process based on the past karmas and the flow of nature's energies. Based on these thoughts, we would normally form new opinions by endorsing or rejecting thoughts that are coming through the karmic pipeline. However, now with the understanding that the mind is a source of bondage, we can rather observe it and make the inner effort to simply observe the thoughts as they come and go. This way, we do not bind the karmas attached to likes, dislikes and opinions.

"Holistic Inner Science" Is Worth Understanding

Questioner – If we do not want to clash, but if the other person comes to pick a fight, then what should be done? In that case, one is alert, but if the other person fights then conflicts surely happens right?

Dadashri – If someone fights with a wall, how long will that fight last? If the head accidentally bangs the wall one day, then what can we do to or with the wall? The head got banged so we screamed at the wall, so what beat–up the wall? Similarly, if they are causing tremendous conflicts they are all like brick walls! In this, what is to be seen of the other person?! We just need to understand *within* ourselves that this person is like a brick wall, this is to be *comprehended*. Then, there is no trouble.

Questioner – If we stay silent then the other one gets the wrong impression that we are at fault somehow and the conflict compounds and escalates.

Dadashri – This is just assumption on your part that I remained silent so as a result this ended up happening. If someone gets up in the middle of the night to go to the "bathroom" and hits a wall in the dark, did they hit the wall because we remained silent?

Whether you stay silent or talk it does not even touch them, it has no bearing whatsoever. By remaining silent the other person gets affected is a misnomer or even by talking the other person gets affected is a misnomer as well. "*ONLY SCIENTIFIC CIRCUMSTANTIAL EVIDENCE*", it is purely the coming together of *scientific evidences*. No one has even the slightest bit of power in or over this. In a world without even the slightest bit of personal power, in that what can anyone do? If the wall has power then they have power! And the chaos that is going to happen instrumentally by this person is not going to let go, what is the point of senselessly panicking? That person has no power or control over his own behavior in this! Hence, why do you not, too, become like a brick wall as well?! If you harass your spouse repeatedly then the God within the spouse keeps a tally that this person is harassing me; and likewise when the spouse harasses you back then you become like a brick wall as well, then the God within will "*help*" you.

Insights From Pearl #51

This is such a deep concept explained with such a beautiful simple example! We tend to make assumptions about other people's behavior, especially when we have difficulties with people. We try to find *cause-effect* with the indirect light of our perverse intellect. It really does not work this way at all. We must understand that each and every individual is spinning like a top to the tune of their own karmas. Due to over-sensitivity, we get *wrongfully* affected. This is where we go wrong and suffer needlessly.

We cannot control the behavior of anybody else. Our goal is not to hurt any living being through our mind-speech-body and to avoid clashes while adjusting everywhere. However, there is fine line. We can only be responsible for our *own* behavior. As long as we know in our hearts that our intention is to settle amicably and not to harm the other person, we must leave the rest to *"scientific circumstantial evidence"*. We wrongly believe we have power over the coming together of evidences in making things happen in the world. In reality, none of us do. We cannot misuse this fact by any means. That would lead to further bondage and suffering. Hence, through awareness and understanding is the way to truly experience holistic inner science *"as it is"* for what it is *exactly*.

PEARL #52

With The Breaking Of Conflict A Publicly Admired Status

Questioner – Even if we do not want to if the other person comes and rants then what?

Dadashri – Yes, this namely is the world right! That is why I am telling you, that find such a *"special hiding place"* that no one has ever known and that no one will ever find, find such a *"special place"*. In this, from anywhere people will find you and make you have conflicts, if not in the middle of the night two mosquitoes will even come and create conflict for you! They will not let you rest! Hence, after coming into the human life form, if you do not want to fall to a lower life form, then do not allow conflicts to happen. Once your conflicts are broken then you help others break theirs so you can be said to have attained a publicly revered status.

Insights From Pearl #52

What our inner state is what projects outwardly. When we have mastered conflict resolution, we become models for others to help resolve their own inner conflicts as well. Public admiration is not something that can be bought. It just happens due what our inner state emanates; the aura that our inner state infuses around us. All human beings have hearts to feel the vibrations that emanate from us. When the vibrations are pure, then the aura, too, becomes something that spontaneously permeates the ether in the surrounding area of that person. When there is true inner peace, wisdom of experience and divine knowledge actively at work *within*; it is not something that requires words or expression, it just *is* a state of *being*.

PEARL #53

Where There Is Positive Intent, There Are No Conflicts

If conflict–filled intentions are not decreasing day–by–day, then human–ness disappears, animal–like state remains.

This 'Akram Marg' is such a path that conflict–filled intentions can be overcome. Hostile intent just cannot stay; it is such a path that hostile intentions can disappear totally. So, there is no conflict left in oneself, and conflicts will not arise in others because of you either; and if another is burning in conflict, due to our non–hostile inner intentions, they too will cool down; the whole intentions undergo a transformation! This 'building' can never be of a hostile intent; because of one's own hostile intentions it appears that the building too is hostile. Then they will say I am not comfortable in this "room". One's own hostile intentions are projected such that everything gets ruined.

If hostile, conflict–filled intentions disappear then even the physical body will become worthy of *puja* to people that is how this world is! Then, it does not matter what you are or your religious faith, whoever has *exhausted–out* all conflict–filled, hostile intentions from within will become famed amongst the public!

Real inner self effort (*purusharth*) only happens after '*gyan*', after which one sits in the 'seat of one's own Pure Soul' so conflict–filled inner intentions gradually decrease; if not before '*gyan*' one conflict–filled intent is removed and four new ones sneak in! Until–and–unless we do not have a "guard" to keep other conflict–filled intentions from slipping in all the myriad neuroses make their way in and when do we encounter a "guard"? When one becomes a "*Purush*", all the power of discretion is according to one's own will. If there is no "guard" then four new conflicts slip in from the back door, so where is the profit in this?

To have an absolute indifference to conflict–filled intentions (*kalushit–bhav*) is in itself liberation (*moksha*)! When hostile inner intent just simply does not arise, from that point it can be considered that the status of the *Lord* has been attained, furthermore if hostile inner intent absolutely disappears then even through their instrumental presence others will not have hostile inner–intent, which can be considered divine!

Insights From Pearl #53

When we wake in the morning, mid-day and in the evening before sleeping for the night, we can reinforce our conviction that "with the present mind-speech-body may there not be even the slightest bit of pain whatsoever to any living being" and repeat it five times, three times per day. If our intention is clear and sincere from the heart center, it will feed into the universal cosmic computer that this is our intent and at some point either in this lifetime or another, the results of these intentions will surely manifest. This is what we are projecting from within so it is up to nature's forces to manifest our inner intentions. We, as humans, are blessed with the incredible power of intention. This is why liberation from the cycle of birth-and-death can only be attained from the human life form. Hostility breeds hostility; non-violence breeds non-violence. Peace, harmony, wisdom, bliss, true affection can only be found where there is non-violent positive intentions.

So, if we are fortunate enough to be self-realized through the grace of the *Gyani Purush*, we are able to develop our indifference to conflict-filled intentions through correct understanding and the quest for inner bliss.

PEARL #54

As Negative Intentions Exhaust Totally, The Person Becomes Revered By Everyone

The soul is itself an absolutely divine pure soul (*Paramatma*) only. So, it is divine, it is *fame–worthy*, but the physical body, too, is such that can attain fame–worthy status but if all the hostile inner intentions get exhausted out! If there are no inner intentions of conflict remaining within one and because of others inner intentions of conflict do not arise within oneself either, then the physical body too becomes fame–worthy! Even when others have conflict-filled inner intentions one does not oneself get infused with conflict-filled intentions then the body (*pudgal*) too becomes fame-worthy. Other inner-intentions may still be present, but the conflict-filled inner intentions should not arise. Oneself, to others, when even an inkling of conflict-filled inner intentions ceases to arise, then famed status happens. "We", what did we see in ourselves? What was it that totally escaped from within us? Why has our body become an instrument of fame with the public? "Ourself" we are incessantly "in our own real self" only but the body has exhausted itself totally of all inner conflict-filled intentions as well! That is why this body has become an instrument of fame! Just the inner conflict-filled intentions have gone and eating, drinking beverages, wearing clothes is still in full force! Actually! Even while wearing polyester clothes, a publicly famed status has been attained! This, too, is a miracle of this age! This is called a paradoxical *puja*, unique and a wonder of the world that has manifested!

Insights From Pearl #54

The *Gyani Purush* truly is the ultimate wonder of the Wonders of the World! He cannot be understood with the reflected light of our intellect alone. We must open our hearts to Him to fully understand and benefit from the amazing presence of a *Gyani Purush* on our earth. He is not interested in fame, but it just happens *naturally*. He never loses His divine humility or divine nature due to this fame either. He is forever firmly planted in His inner bliss as the observer from within. He does not crave respect, fame or status, but rather simply *is* divinity in human form. His divine fragrance and grace spreads *effortlessly* as He is incessantly in a divine inner state of being.

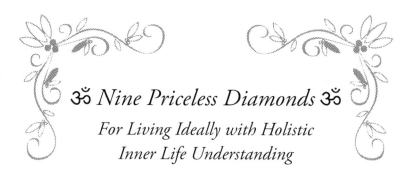

ॐ *Nine Priceless Diamonds* ॐ

For Living Ideally with Holistic Inner Life Understanding

№ 1

O Supreme Self! May you bless me with such an infinite inner strength as would restrain me from hurting, causing someone to hurt or supporting someone hurting even slightly, the ego of any living being.

Bless me with such an infinite inner strength in the philosophy of relative pluralism in thinking, speech, and conduct as would restrain me from hurting even slightly, the ego of any living being.

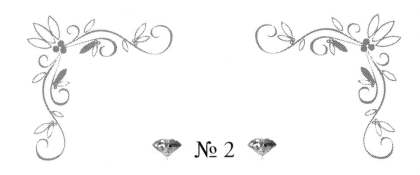

 № 2

O Supreme Self! May you bless me with
such an infinite inner strength so as not
to hurt, neither cause someone to hurt
nor support someone hurting even to
the slightest extent, the basis or viewpoint of any religion faith and beliefs.

May you bless me with such an
infinite inner strength in the
philosophy of relative pluralism in
speech, conduct and thinking as
would restrain me from hurting any
religious view-points or beliefs.

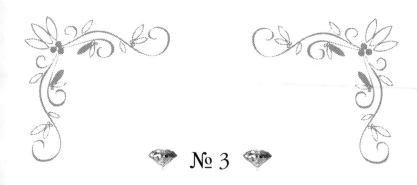

№ 3

O Supreme Self! May you bless me
with such an infinite inner strength
as would restrain me from uttering
untrue adverse things, from offending
or showing disregards to any preacher,
monk, nun or a religious head.

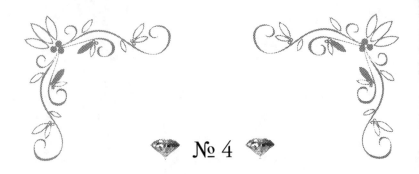

№ 4

O Supreme Self! May you bless me with such an infinite inner strength as would not make me dislike or hate any living being to the slightest extent, neither cause anyone nor support anyone doing so.

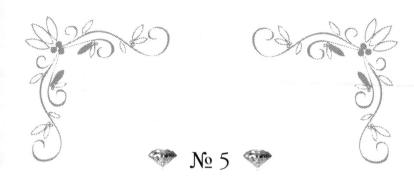

№ 5

O Supreme Self! May you bless me
with such an infinite inner strength
as would restrain me from speaking,
causing to speak, or supporting someone
speaking harsh, hurtful language
or obstinate language to anyone.

Kindly give me inner strength to
speak soft, sober, soothing language
even if someone speaks harsh, hurtful,
egoistic or biting language.

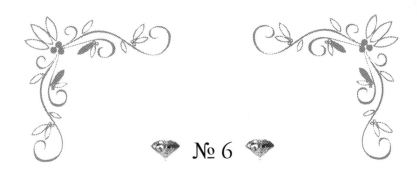

№ 6

O Supreme Self! May you bless me
with such an infinite inner strength
as would restrain me having faults,
desires, gestures or thoughts of perverted
sensuality or passion towards any
gender – male, female or neuter.

Kindly give me the supreme strength
so as to be free of sensual or passionate
attitudes or perversions forever.

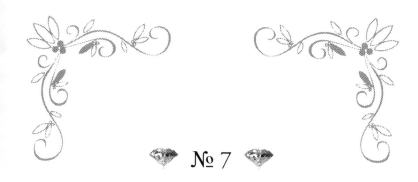

№ 7

O Supreme Self! May you bless me
with such an infinite inner strength
to control my excessive temptation
towards any relish or taste of food.

Give me the strength to take food
having balance of all tastes.

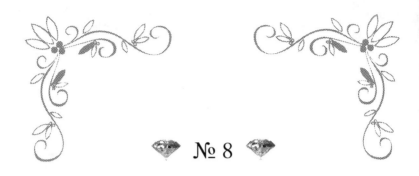

№ 8

O Supreme Self! May you bless me with such an infinite inner strength as would restrain me from uttering untrue adverse things, from offending or showing disregard towards any being – living or dead, in one's presence or absence.

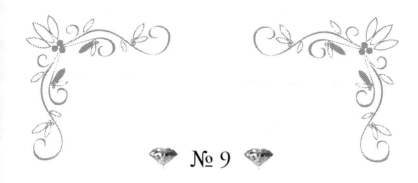

№ 9

O Supreme Self! May you bless me
with such an infinite inner strength
for being instrumental in welfare of
the world that is for the common
good of mankind as a whole.

Infinite Power to the Bliss of the Supreme Self!

Valuable Summary by Dr. Shailesh Mehta, Opthamologist, Vadodara, Gujarat, India

---

Today progress of physical or material sciences has gifted us all with abundance of luxuries and comforts. But if we look within, don't we have inner unrest, disputes, clashes and difficulty of adjustments with each other? Do we need to know art and science of happy, harmonious, rich and meaningful inner living?

What takes away my inner happiness and harmony? Inner and outer clashes and conflicts do play major role. A home should be a heaven on earth but it becomes a testing place for us. All interpersonal dealings get tainted by conflicts and lack of adjustment.

Why do conflicts or clashes occur even though no one really wants them to occur? It is due to sheer ignorance.

In previous times people used to have understanding that if we find faults, put allegations or blames and shout at family members, they would be hurt. Today right on a dining table war starts, "you did this and you did that." Where there are clashes, there is a lack of correct understanding, no human-ness

Everyone feels 'I am right, why he or she does not understand?' Well, I have right to put forward my view point and I can explain or persuade but no sooner I become adamant or insistent,it will result in to clashes. I need to know and remain aware that everyone is right by his or her own view point. Everyone having passed through different life situations may have different understanding, different inner development and different inner environment too. So it is natural to have different perceptions or different viewpoints but it should not result into disputes, conflicts or clashes.

Commonsense is one which is applicable everywhere theoretically and practically. It will resolve any situation such that minds will not get apart. The master holistic guide says, "Decide to avoid clashes and inner light will show you the way how to sail through the situation without having any clashes." Even if someone provokes there should not be clashes from our side. If one can understand intention and point of view of other person things would become easy.

We also should know that every one may have different revolutions that is to say speed of understanding and comprehension may be different for everyone. How can a motor with 500 revolutions per minute match with one having 5000 rpm. It is duty of one having higher revolutions to put counter pulley or come down to level of one having lower ones.

We humans expect others to be like us. We view and evaluate with our design, our spectacles. In previous times there were farms whereas in present times there are gardens at home and workplace. In a farm there is one crop, all wheat or rice, all alike whereas in a garden all tress or plants are different but none without a fruit or a flower. Does a rose plant tell to a mango tree, "Why you do not have a flower?" And mango never says to a rose plant "why you do not have a fruit like me?" All humans have different fruits and flowers in terms of skills or positivity. So find and make best use of what one knows and never complain about shortcomings.

Clashes lead to loss of inner harmony; inner strength and can even lead to animosity. Modern science and medical science researches do endorse that unresolved conflicts or clashes lead to lots of stress, detrimental hormonal and neurological effects on mind, body and consciousness. Many present day diseases are related to conflicts, clashes and stresses.

'Avoid clashes 'is the golden key. If one knows only this much one can straight away reach to the doorstep of liberation. One even may not need a guru or a guide.

One needs to win one's own home and world need not be conquered. A home with good, warm mutual dealings can be a heaven right here. One should have love and care for each other.

The spousal union is a precious relationship. Like in a business, here also one should be careful in dealing with a partner. It should be like best friends. But even after a marriage two 'I' remain separate. As long as one 'I' is loving, sharing and caring for the other 'I' it is win-win situation. But if one 'I' tries to win over the other, difficulties start. One should use words like we or ours and not like I and you or mine and yours.

If I try to make him or her happy, first I would be happy and if the other is hurt, I would also be disturbed first. If understood correctly he or she is me only.

Hiraba, wife of Master Holistic Guide Mr. A.M. Patel lost her one eye in young age. People started asking him if he would like to remarry. He replied, "I have promised to care for her in presence of sacred fire and I would live this whole life to keep my promise. So even if she loses her second eye, I would care for her."

Where there is love no faults are kept notes of. What is believed to be love in worldly language is merely infatuation with give and take conditions. Love is one which is free of expectations and conditions. It would remain constant and not having waxing or waning.

Ultimately one should live such that karmic bonds with spouse or other family members are settled amicably with equanimity and certainly new adverse bonds should not be generated.

Dealing with children also seems to be a tough test. Children do not listen to us or walk the way we may not like. How to handle the children?

The Master Holistic Guide has given many fold pearls of wisdom. A major one is 'Glass handle with care.' We handle parcel with such a label very carefully and even if angry do not throw it. Likewise we have to handle mind of children. Children seek love. They learn what they see and not what we say them. Responsibility of parents is more than a president of a country. Character of parents is of paramount importance. We have to nourish them like a gardener, allowing them to blossom naturally. We should explain things scientifically such that they can see for themselves benefits and losses, bright and dark sides of everything. But forcible enforcement may not bring good results.

As children we also have duties towards our parents. Service and care of parents stand highest in the world. It is inhumane to leave parents alone especially in time of need.

This guide book provides good insight and pearls of wisdom for making our own home clash-free and brimming with true joy from the heart centers of everyone in the home.

Glossary

Abhinivesha – persistence, stubbornness

Adharma – absence of heart-centered inner humane living

Adhi – tension, worry, anxiety

Ahamkar – misguided relative illusory ego

Akram marg – step-less path to liberation

Ashriit – protected by nature

Asmita – ego, selfishness

Avidya – ignorance

Avyabichiarini – balanced and positive (intellect)

Bhabhi – sister-in-law

Bhagavan – 100% human

Bharat – place of light, another name for India

Chai – Indian tea

Dada – emancipated divine state in a living human body

Dharma – heart-centered inner humane living

Dwesha – hate, aversion, disdain

Ghee – refined butter with fat removed

Guru – religious guide

Gyan – eternal knowledge

Gyani Purush – Holistic scientist capable of enabling a non-realized person to become self-realized through His grace, compassion and unmatchable spiritual prowess

Kalushit-bhav – conflict-ridden intention

Kankaas – disturbing interaction

Karuna – compassion

Kaviraj – composer/singer of poetic hymns

Kaviraj paado – poetic hymns of the poet

Kirtan bhakti – highest form of devotion, direct devotion

Klesha – distressing conflict, taints, afflictions

Krupa – grace

Kshaitriya – warrior class in hierarchy of original four classes in India

Ladoo – Indian sweet ball

Moha – illusory infatuation

Mukti – inner freedom

Moksha – ultimate liberation

Moksha dharma – path leading to ultimate liberation

Namaskar – salutation to the soul within

Naav-kalamo – Nine Priceless Diamonds

Nirashriit – unprotected by nature

Pakodas – Indian batter-fried vegetables

Paramatma – the absolute observer within

Patanjali – maharishi Patanjali who composed the yoga sutras in sanskrit originally

Pudgal – non-soul matter

Puja – religious/spiritual ritual

Purush – the supreme self

Purusharth – introspective real inner effort

Raga – attachment to pleasure, fear of change

Saavdhan – gentle carefulness

Sansar – worldly relative life

Samay varte savdhaan – gentle carefulness at critical times

Shanti – peace

Shashtras – Indian scriptures

Surya Narayan Dev – Sun God

Taap – penance

Tyaag – renunciation

Tri-mantra – triple mantra bringing all religions together, mantra for removing obstacles

Vyabichairini – perverted (intellect)

Reader's Holistic Insights